NEW TESTAMENT TITHE OR SATANIC TRICK?

Terry Cleveland

Published by Terry Cleveland, 2023.

NEW TESTAMENT TITHE OR SATANIC TRICK?

First edition. August 22, 2023.

Copyright © 2023 Terry Cleveland.

ISBN: 979-8218093822

Written by Terry Cleveland.

DEDICATED

To those who like myself grew up being led astray by bad religious traditions and commandments of men inspired by satanic influence. To all who unwittingly accepted a counterfeit of Christianity and need to be reminded that God has said "Return to Me and I will return to you" (Mal. 3:7).

INTRODUCTION

For many years the people of earth thought the sun revolved around the planets. Everyone thought so because everyone said so. But they were all wrong. Nothing is true simply because everyone says it's true.

For many years the people of earth thought the earth was flat. It was said if you went too far out you would fall off the edge. Everyone thought it was flat because everyone said it was flat. But they were all wrong. Nothing is true simply because everyone thinks it's true.

For many years people have been using (OT) Old Testament Tithe law in the (NT) New Testament Church. Doing this because many others have been doing this for so long. But they are all wrong. Nothing is the right thing to do in the Lord's Church simply because it's been done for a long time.

What man says and does is not the most important. What God says and does is always the most important. Could there be a NT tithe that only protithers know about? Unknown to Father God, Lord Jesus, and NT scripture? Or is this another satanic lie? Another ploy designed to give advantage to the one who **"deceives the whole world" (Rev. 12:9)**? Do you understand how important it is that you know the truth?

Lord Jesus said, **"If you abide in My word, you are My disciples indeed. And you shall know the truth, and the truth shall make you free" (John 8:31,32).**

. . . .

1

ONE

THE TRUTH

· · · ·

"God is Spirit, and those who worship Him
must worship in spirit and truth."
(John 4:24)

MANY ANCIENT PEOPLE: Romans, Babylonians, Assyrians and others adopted systems that used a tenth percentage of their possessions as the standard amount for certain negotiations: political, religious, and otherwise. They all adopted some form of what became known as the Tithe among the Hebrews, the ancient Israelites.

For others the tenth or tenths were used similarly as payment of tax, for tribute, for contributions and such. But the religious tithing system of the Hebrews involved their God, His Priesthood, and their growing nation. Because of the many changes made as the nation grew their system is the most difficult for the people of today to understand. What began as one voluntary tithe became three or four that were **"according to the law" (Heb. 7:5).** Those who received God's tithes and where they received them also changed over time.

Israel's ancient Covenant Code (Ex. 23:16,19) says nothing about a tithe. It speaks only of offerings for the God of the Hebrews. However, many years later, having been made law, the Deuteronomic Code demanded a tithe of crops.

· · · ·

3

NT TITHE?

During the reigns of Kings David and Solomon the tax and the tithe were ten percent by law. We know the tithe was not always law because Abram, patriarch of the Hebrew nation, when meeting Melchizedek, King of Salem (Jerusalem) and Priest of God Most High **"gave him tithe of all"** (Gen. 14:18-20). Abram lived centuries before his people became a nation and received God's law at Mount Sinai.

As their nation grew and the needs of the people expanded so did the number and uses of the tithes. Along with the tithe being made law came God's laws for tithing. Laws that were established for God's chosen people only. The only people given God's command to tithe and collect tithes (Heb. 7:5).

Those ancient tithe laws, given only to the children of Israel, have been twisted and used by the powers of darkness to deceive the NT Church. Satan's false teachers have convinced people they are supposed to tithe because they serve the same God that tithing Israel served.

Not true! Not true! Not true! In Holy scripture Father God reveals His intimate relationships are based on individual legal contracts known as Covenants and Testaments. And as Sovereign of all contracts His judgements are always judiciously legal. It's not legal that one must do something because it's in someone else's covenant. Each is an individual covenant.

Especially not legal when that other covenant has been rejected by Father God. **"In that He says, "A new covenant, "He has made the first obsolete"** (Heb. 8:13). Father's judicial involvement is always according to covenant and dispensation. **"Shall not the Judge of all the earth do right?"** (Gen 18:25).

4

THE TRUTH

The satanic powers of darkness will use anything and everything they can to confuse and mislead the church of Christ. They are trying to prolong the kingdom of the evil one. They use the OT laws of the obsolete Mosaic covenant (Gal. 3:24,25) like fiery darts. The tithe is one of those OT laws (Heb. 7:5) used as a fiery dart, thrown with the hand of religious tradition. And not only the tithe, but the devil has tried to sneak every OT law he could into the NT Church.

Why? Because the Word of God says **"the (OT) law is not of faith, but "the man who does them shall live by them" (Gal. 3:12).** The acceptance of any faithless OT law hurts the church today. And the passing on of such bad religious traditions will hurt the church tomorrow.

If we allow satan to trick us into using the doctrine of the expired OT in the NT Church, what shall we do with the doctrine Father gave (John 7:16) the NT Church? The doctrine that Lord Jesus, by giving His life, established in our covenant for us?

Because people think the tithe is NT doctrine, they don't consider the results of using OT law in the NT Church. To have a good understanding of anything you must know the whole truth. Although protithers disagree, the tithe is not NT doctrine. It is the doctrine of the OT covenant of law (Deut. 14).

Once this fact is understood, along with the rules of covenant, it is easier to see the devil's trick. Many people have been NT tithing for a long time thinking it's of God. I was once one of them. But the NT tithe is a fake! The work of **"that serpent of old, called the Devil and Satan, who deceives the whole world; he was cast to the earth" (Rev. 12:9).**

NEW TESTAMENT TITHE OR SATANIC TRICK?   5

NT TITHE?

The book of Deuteronomy states **"One witness shall not rise against a man concerning any iniquity or sin that he commits; by the mouth of two or three witnesses the matter shall be established"** **(Deut. 19:15).** Although the bible has many witnesses to the fact, we will look to three of the most authoritative witnesses to see what they say about the tithe being OT doctrine or NT doctrine.

For our first witness we look to the words of Lord Jesus, the One Father God sent to redeem the world from OT law (Gal. 4:4,5). He said **"Woe to you, scribes and pharisees, hypocrites! For you pay tithe of mint and anise and cumin, and you have neglected the weightier matters of the law; justice, mercy and faith"** **(Matt. 23:23).** Here Lord Jesus scolds them for only doing the easy part of the law, the tithe. But not the weightier parts of the law. In this our Lord acknowledges the tithe to be OT law and therefore it cannot be NT doctrine.

Our second witness is Moses, the mediator of the Mosaic covenant, the human author of the Pentateuch, the first five books of the covenant of law. In the fifth book of the Law, Deuteronomy, is one of the most important laws given to the ancient Israelites. **"At the end of every seven years, at the appointed time in the year of release, at the Feast of Tabernacles, when all Israel comes to appear before the Lord your God in the place He chooses, you shall read this law before all Israel in their hearing"** **(Deut. 31:11).** This book rehearses all the laws of the covenant of law. Deuteronomy (14:22-29) is just one of its many instructions for tithing. This witness also confirms the tithe to be OT law, not NT doctrine.

THE TRUTH

Lord Jesus says the tithe is OT law, and therefore cannot be NT doctrine (Matt. 23:23). The mediation of Moses confirms this with the many instructions for tithing recorded only in the Mosaic covenant of law. But nowhere in the bible is as much explained about the tithe as with our third witness.

Our third witness is the witness of witnesses, the great witness, the one tithe lovers hate. They wish they could take this out of the bible. This is the smoking gun, the witness that tells what some protithers try to hide. Our third witness, (Hebrews 7:5) gives more information about the tithe than any other single passage of scripture in the bible. It tells who was supposed to tithe. Who was supposed to receive the tithe? By whose authority it was to be collected. And it gives the identification of the only people the tithe laws were given to.

"And indeed, those who are the sons of Levi, who receive the priesthood, have a commandment to receive tithes from the people according to the law, that is from their brethren, though they have come from the loins of Abraham" (Heb. 7:5). Many people are led astray by not knowing this.

This is the truth, the whole truth, and nothing but the truth concerning the tithe. The Levitical priesthood, and only the Levitical priesthood was given a command by Father God, the only one who could command His priesthood, to collect His tithes (Lev. 27:30) from His people. Which means the tithing system, like the Levitical priesthood, was a system within the Judaic faith, not the Christian faith. Agreeing with the words of Christ, and the writings of Moses, our third witness states the tithe was **"according to the (OT) law" (Heb. 7:5).**

7

NT TITHE?

Did the command from God for His priesthood to receive His tithes include the NT Church? No, when Father gave the command for His priesthood to collect His tithes there was no NT Church. It was hundreds of years in the future. The tithing system, though originated by the Hebrews, was made law and developed for the good of the Hebrew people by Father God.

The tithing system, our third witness explains, by the inclusion of only the Levitical priesthood and their brethren, was exclusively for those who came **"from the loins of Abraham" (Heb. 7:5).** It was for those of the Judaic faith. The faith developed in and encompassing all aspects of the Mosaic covenant of law. Not the Christian faith, developed in the love and sacrifice of Christ, as seen clearly by His Cross.

Because the tithe is OT law, established before the coming of Christ, it is not based on faith. **"Yet the (OT) law is not of faith, but the man who does them shall live by them" (Gal. 3:12). "But before faith came, we were kept under guard by the law, kept for the faith which would afterward be revealed. Therefore, the law was our tutor to bring us to Christ, that we might be justified by faith. But after faith has come, we are no longer under a tutor" (Gal. 3:23-25).**

No longer should anyone be under OT law because, **"when the fullness of time had come, God sent forth His Son, born of a woman, born under the law, to redeem those who were under the law, that we might receive the adoption as sons" (Gal. 4:4,5).** Protithers are successful in recruiting people to become tithers who don't know Christ's death redeemed all from OT law. And those who don't know the tithe is OT law (Heb. 7:5).

THE TRUTH

Protithers, to satan's advantage, are passing on to others the bad religious traditions they received from those who taught them. Many of these false teachers are not intentionally trying to fool anyone. They are false teachers simply because they mistakenly accepted false doctrine. Believing those they thought knew the truth they accepted their teachings, which turned out to be bad religious traditions, not biblical facts.

Right or wrong people usually teach what they were taught. And as a result of passing on what they thought God said, instead of what God really said, many have become victims of the satanically inspired bad religious tradition of doing the OT tithe in their Church. A true NT Church has no tithe.

Many of man's bad religious traditions were planted in satan's fake Roman Church. They grew there and after becoming tradition were transplanted to deceived people in the Church of Christ. This is how satan tricked the NT Church, not only to accept his fake NT tithe, but also the ancient pagan festival that honored the idol gods of the fertility cults, known as Easter. It was in this same fake church of Rome, satan's church, that God's law of a tithe of food (**"that there may be food in My house" (Mal. 3:10)** was changed for a tithe of money.

There are no instructions for the NT Church to tithe anywhere in NT scriptures. Nor is it recorded anywhere in NT scripture that a NT Church, any NT Church, ever taught tithing, received tithes, paid tithes, or ever had anything to do with tithing! The system of tithing was for ancient Israel, God's special people only. That's why the instructions for tithing are recorded in the scriptures of the Old Testament only.

NT TITHE?

The claim that the NT Church is obligated to obey OT laws is satanic. It is one of the longest lasting deceptions in history. It led many NT people to think they were supposed to tithe. It is not true. The OT Mosaic law **"was added because of transgressions, till the seed (Christ) should come to whom the promise was made" (Gal. 3:19).** And just as Father God, through His prophets, told the people of the OT what He expected them to do, He did the same for the people of the NT. But He never told them to tithe. The tithe was to be used until Christ came.

The satanic heresy called the NT tithe is the most diabolically sinister lie the powers of darkness has ever infested the NT Church with. The unholy trinity, satan, and the beast from the sea, and the beast from the earth (Rev. 13) infested the early NT Church with various OT laws. They knew changing the tithe from food to money in their church would be spread by false teachers and greed. They wanted Christ's Church to fail.

This satanic heresy is being used in satan's attempt to turn the true church of Christ into the church of satan. Fearing the power of Christ's resurrection and its spread to all Christians, satan is trying to stop people from becoming Christians and receiving the power of the new covenant. Satan knows the bible says, **"the (OT) law is not of faith, but "the man who does them shall live by them" (Gal. 3:12).** Those whom he has tricked into using OT law, whether they know it or not, are living by faithless OT law (Gal. 3:11). And therefore, only think they are Christians. Their having accepted satan's counterfeit of Christianity, has robbed them of NT Holy Spirit power. The thing satan fears most and tries his best to stop.

10

THE TRUTH

False teachers love to quote Malachi (3:10) **"Bring all the tithes into the storehouse".** They quote it every Sunday while collecting fake tithes. They boldly quote it just as if it was NT scripture and NT doctrine. People have been hearing this in Churches for so long they think it is NT scripture and NT doctrine. It is not. It is scripture from the old obsolete Judaic covenant. The covenant that was replaced over two thousand years ago when our great shepherd, Lord Jesus, gave His life to give the world a better covenant, (Heb. 8:6). It's the New Covenant that gives the NT Church it's instructions, not the old.

People become tithers because they have believed satan's lie that the tithe is what all people owe God. The ancient Israelites owed Father God His tithe. That they turn over to Him ten percent of all harvests was part of their covenant (Deut. 14:22). Father gave them ninety percent of all harvests but the ten percent He retained for His own use. To feed His Priesthood and for other reasons as needed. **"And all the tithe of the land, whether of the seed or of the fruit of the tree, is the Lord's. It is holy to the Lord"** (Lev. 27:30). It belonged to God.

Their covenant was a covenant of law because they were in rebellion against the rule of God. And Father God, having chosen them as a people of His own, for His own special purposes, was using law to bring them out of their pagan ways so they could become the people He had called them to be. For four hundred and thirty years they lived among pagan people and had in fact become pagan people themselves. Long forgotten were the teachings of their forefathers. Both God and Israel needed to trust each other, it started with the tithe law.

NT TITHE?

But ours is a different situation and a different people. We are the children of God whom He has adopted into His family. Made possible by the sacrifice of God's only begotten Son, our Lord who loves us and gave Himself for us. He took our sins and gave us His righteousness. The ancient Israelites owed Father God His tithe which He used to help them. But we, God's New Covenant children **"have been given all things that pertain to life and godliness"** (2 Pet. 1:3). **"He who did not spare His own Son, but delivered Him up for us all, how shall He not with Him also freely give us all things?"** (Rom. 8:32). These things pertain to God's children, who have been given not ninety percent, but all. Like Father, we give from love not debt.

You can rant and rave and jump up and down declaring you are a child of God. But God's word says if you do OT law, and the tithe is OT law (Heb. 7:5), you are not a child of God, you cannot be a Christian. **"But that no one is justified by the (OT) law in the sight of God is evident, for "the just shall live by faith. "Yet the (OT) law is not of faith, but the man who does them shall live by them"** (Gal. 3:11,12).

People having the same power that raised Lord Jesus from death is what satan is trying to stop. For people to just think they are Christians, yet live without the power of the Holy Spirit, is the aim of the devil. These are no threat to him, and they mislead others to think you can be a Christian and not have power. But our Lord said, **"you shall receive power when the Holy Spirit has come upon you"** (Acts 1:8). When people understand the NT, they know the reason satan tries to stop people from being Christians is Holy Spirit power.

THE TRUTH

Satan always crafts his tricks and heresies around the Word of God. It's not the Word of God that gives satan what he wants, he gets what he wants by getting people to violate the Word of God. He usually does this by using his favorite weapons, lies. He continues to lie about OT law. OT law was added **"because of transgressions (Gal. 3:19)** to help until Christ came. Satan, with the fake tithe, is lying to the people of the NT Church that this OT law was meant for them also.

But the use of OT law in the NT Church is the rejection of NT law, the law of Christ. Which, when considering the price Christ paid to establish the NT law, is a very serious offense. A very serious offense to God the Father who sent Him. And a very serious offense to God the Son who came and gave His life to establish a New Covenant and New Covenant law.

For the first three hundred years of the NT Church there was no such thought as a NT tithe. No tithe is mentioned in the recorded actions of any church in the book of Acts. There is no mention of a tithe in any of the appeals for financial help for the struggling churches in Jerusalem doing the famine (1 and 2 Cor.). From its very beginning the NT Church operated according to the doctrine Lord Jesus received from Father God. **"Jesus answered them and said, "My doctrine is not Mine, but His who sent Me" (John 7:16).**

What was Father's doctrine for accepting OT offerings? What offering doctrine did He give the NT Church? We can go to the first recorded offerings Father accepted to see the doctrine He uses. We will find the answer to both questions because as He said, **"I am the Lord, I do not change" (Mal. 3:6).**

NT TITHE?

The very first offering Father God received was for the building of the Sanctuary in the wilderness. From the Sanctuary to the Temple, to the NT Church, our God does not change. **"Then the Lord spoke to Moses, saying: "Speak to the children of Israel, that they bring Me an offering. From everyone who gives it willingly with his heart you shall take My offering" (Ex. 25:1,2).** The word translated "willing" is the Hebrew word "Nadab" which means to volunteer, and voluntarily. NT scripture says the same thing, **"So let each one give as he purposes in his heart, not grudgingly or of necessity; for God loves a cheerful giver" (2 Cor. 9:7).** The key word is Heart.

"And Moses spoke to all the congregation of the children of Israel, saying, "This is the thing which the Lord commanded, saying: "Take from among you an offering to the Lord. Whoever is of a willing heart, let him bring it as an offering to the Lord" (Ex. 35:4,5). In this second recorded offering received by Father God we see again the word "willing", the Hebrew word "Nadab" meaning to volunteer.

This is the doctrine Father God gave Lord Jesus for receiving offerings in the NT Church. And this can be seen throughout the scriptures of the NT. No one is supposed to tell you what you are to give in the NT Church. There is no authority above Almighty God who says what you give should come from your willing heart. The bible calls it Free Will Offerings.

The NT Church is God's family of Christ like volunteers. Doing for the love of Him who first loved us and gave Himself for us as a ransom for many. Nothing is to be done grudgingly (reluctantly) or of necessity (being compelled to do), (2 Cor. 9:7).

THE TRUTH

The satanic powers of darkness, through false teachers and religious traditionalists, use the fake NT tithe to rob the children of God. They are robbed of the many blessings that would have been theirs with covenant obedience. But when you do OT law, any OT law, you are living by OT law which is without faith, and therefore outside of your covenant, (Gal. 3:12), (Lev. 18:5). Living by that which is without faith disqualifies you from receiving everything that is to be gained by faith.

Why do you think so many Churches teach and preach the OT tithe yet claim to be a NT Church? When they never teach or preach Father's number one offerings doctrine (Ex. 25:2), (2 Cor. 9:7) volunteerism? Volunteerism is the very essence of what makes the NT the better covenant it is (Heb. 8:6). To establish the New Covenant Father God volunteered His only begotten Son (John 3:16). Lord Jesus volunteered Himself (John 10:18). Father volunteered His Holy Spirit (Acts 1:4). And true Christians voluntarily accept the Spirit and wisdom of the NT.

Can a church really be a NT Church and ignore the doctrine of the NT, and use the doctrine of the OT? Why would anyone turn down the very best there is, the NT, (Heb. 8:6) to accept what use to be, the OT (Heb. 8:13). There can be only one reason. Because they have been deceived. **"So the great dragon was cast out, that serpent of old, called the devil and satan, who deceives the whole world" (Rev. 12:9).** Like Adam and Eve protithers think they can get more by listening to deception than by listening to God. Blinded by greed they can't see that anything opposing God cannot be trusted. And everything that leads you to ignore the Word of God is your enemy.

NT TITHE?

Is it alright if people drive their cars using expired tags? Is it alright if they drive with expired driver's license? No. But a great many people who say they love the Lord who gave His life to establish a new and better covenant for them think it's alright for them to serve Him by using the doctrine of the expired Old Covenant (Heb. 8:13), while neglecting the doctrine of the New Covenant when the issue is money.

Some people make money the exception. They know what God has said, and they know Gods Word is true. And they will do whatever they can to follow what they know is the right thing to do on all occasions except when it comes to money. They set Christian ethics aside when it comes to money. There is no greater dishonor to our God than putting Him in second place, when it comes to money, in His house.

16

TWO
WHAT TITHERS DON'T KNOW

· · · ·

**"Wisdom is the principal thing; therefore get wisdom.
And in all your getting, get understanding."**
(Prov. 4:7)

WHEN I WAS GROWING up, I'd hear people say, "What you don't know can't hurt you." I've learned there is no sound reasoning behind that saying. In fact, nothing is farther from the truth. It was something people said simply because other people said it. But the fact of the matter is, as God's Word says, **"My people are destroyed for a lack of knowledge" (Hos. 4:6).** Yes, people die sometimes because of what they don't know. Sometimes they die because of what they think they know.

And sometimes people accept that something is true when it's not. There is something in mankind that makes us always want to go along with the crowd. Having never taken a good look at it for themselves, people will accept that something is true because other people do. Perhaps going along is just easier than going against. Or so it seems.

In many years of bible study and talking to many tithers, having been one myself, I've discovered this to be the case with the use of the OT tithe law in the NT Church. With something as important as financially supporting the work of our Lord in His NT Church, when asked to do so by use of the OT tithe law, people agree because so many others agreed.

17

NT TITHE?

Without taking a biblically informed look at tithing for themselves they agree. They reason, as I also once did, that this must be the right thing to do because so many others have been doing this for so long. But that is just a guess. Because they don't know the tithe is OT law (Heb. 7:5) they have no idea they are putting themselves under a curse (Gal. 3:10).

At first, I thought the same way. I just went along with the crowd and did what everyone else did. I was a tither for over thirty years. For over one hundred and fifty years in America many of those who say they are a NT Church have been using this doctrine from the old obsolete (Heb. 8:13) covenant of Judaism. Because of satan's lying promises of them getting more finance this way, they have been acting on tradition, not bible. And because of their lack of knowledge, they have been doing things just as satan planned. **"The thief does not come except to steal, and to kill, and to destroy" (John 10:10).**

"Enter by the narrow gate; for wide is the gate and broad is the way that leads to destruction, and there are many who go in by it. Because narrow is the gate and difficult is the way which leads to life, and there are few who find it" (Matt. 7:13,14). As my years in church progressed, I began to study the bible more in depth. In those early years of bible study, I received an amazing gift, an insatiable appetite for more bible knowledge. I wanted to know all I could about the one who loved me so much that He was willing to die so I would have a chance to live forever. How could anyone not love Him? And you cannot love Lord Jesus without loving the Word of God because He is the living Word, the true Manna from heaven.

WHAT TITHERS DON'T KNOW

For me every day is another bible adventure, another day in the study of God's Word. With the Holy Spirit as my guide the Word of God has become the daily empowerment that enables my imaginary sojourns through the times and places of the bible (John 3:8). He has taught me to see things I never could before. Which led me to realize some of the things being taught by some people were in fact very different from what the bible said about the same subjects. One thing I found very different from what NT scripture teaches is the OT tithe in the NT Church. NT scriptures show no association of a tithe with the NT Church. Never, nowhere in NT scripture.

When asked to become a tither, those who say yes, say yes to a very bad religious tradition. A tradition inspired by the satanic powers of darkness. Many of the religious traditionalists who ask people to become tithers have good intentions. But when it comes to the truth concerning the tithe, they don't know that they don't know. Most have no knowledge of satan's fake church, his so-called NT Church of Rome. Or of how satan's unholy trinity in his fake church changed the tithe from food to money to sneak this OT law into Christ's Church.

This trick, powered by money, disqualifies people from being Christians by their use of this OT law. **"But that no one is justified by the (OT) law in the sight of God is evident, for "the just shall live by faith. Yet the (OT) law is not of faith, but the man who does them shall live by them" (Gal. 3:11,12).** OT law was known as "the law" because it was the only law Israel ever had until the NT. Those temporary laws, for use only until the coming of Christ, (Gal. 3:19) lasted 1500 years.

19

NT TITHE?

Because of a lack of dedicated study, the kind of study people devote to their smart phones, to their P. C., TV and the like, they don't know there is no such thing as a NT tithe. And it's not just the OT tithe but the use of any OT law disqualifies a person from being a Christian. **"You have become estranged from Christ, you who attempt to be justified by law; you have fallen from grace" (Gal. 5:4).** OT law is out. NT law is in.

Tithers don't know they are putting themselves in the very same position as countless unfortunate others. People who lost their lives for doing the very same thing tithers are doing in the NT Church today. Being unfaithful to their covenant. Tithers don't know they could be tithing themselves to death, doing exactly what satan wants them to do.

"Anyone who has rejected Moses' law dies without mercy on the testimony of two or three witnesses. Of how much worse punishment, do you suppose, will he be thought worthy who has trampled the Son of God underfoot, counted the blood of the covenant by which he was sanctified a common thing, and insulted the Spirit of grace?" (Heb. 10:28,29). When you rather use the OT tithe, a doctrine of an obsolete covenant, than to use the voluntary offerings doctrine of the covenant Christ gave His life to establish for you, you have trampled the Son of God underfoot. You have counted His blood of less value than the blood of the bulls and goats used in the OT. And you have insulted the Spirit of grace. You are ignoring what your covenant says about offerings. You are ignoring the price Christ paid to establish the fulfilled laws (Matt. 5:17) into the NT, the better covenant, established on better promises.

WHAT TITHERS DON'T KNOW

Deceived and being led by the satanically inspired traditions of men, like the vanquished northern tribes of Israel, and like Judah the southern tribes when walking 1000 miles to Babylonian exile, NT tithers will one day ask why. Why were we not doing what our covenant said for us to do? Why, when it came to money, were we using doctrine from the obsolete covenant that once belonged to Judaism, instead of just doing as we were instructed in our own Christian covenant?

Tithers are also disobedient to their covenant because of false teachings by deceived leadership. **"For the leaders of this people cause them to err, and those who are led by them are destroyed" (Is. 9:16).** Many churches have for years been on the receiving end of guidance from leaders who continue to pass on the same bad religious traditions of satan's counterfeit Christianity. Some it seems, just as satan planned, are more interested in saving dollars than people.

Knowing greed to be one of mankind's worse weaknesses, the powers of darkness working in satan's fake Church of Rome changed the defunct OT tithe from food to money in order to trick the NT Church to do this OT law. Satan is more than willing to buy cooperation with money or whatever man desires.

The doctrines on giving and receiving in the NT Church comes from Father God (John 7:16). Lord Jesus taught them to His apostles, who taught them to His Church. The God given doctrines of the NT Church are all recorded in NT scripture. The tithe is OT doctrine (Deut. 14:22-29) taught to NT people by religious traditionalists and those deceived by satan to believe money is more important than the truth of God's Word.

NT TITHE?

Obeying leaders who tell you to do what OT scripture said for the ancient Hebrews to do three thousand years ago, instead of doing what NT scripture says for you to do today, is covenant unfaithfulness. Because of covenant unfaithfulness only two of all adults rescued out of Egypt did not die in the wilderness. Only two were willing to live up to their pledge, **"All that the Lord has said we will do, and be obedient"** (Ex. 24:7). Of that great number of adults only Joshua and Caleb entered the promise land.

People who refuse to live by the doctrine of the NT lead other people into the wilderness of covenant disobedience where their faith, and sometimes they themselves drop dead. **"It is a fearful thing to fall into the hands of the living God" (Heb. 10:31).** Covenant obedience is something tithers don't know. And because they don't know they are at risk.

That next generation of Hebrews that did make it into the promise land made and broke their covenant with the Lord who loved and rescued them, in just a few days. And although the Lord renewed the covenant again and again, they broke it again and again. Finally, Father God refused to renew it again and it was rendered obsolete (Heb. 8:13). This was the covenant that had the tithe and its laws (Deut. 14:22-29). It's the defunct covenant that satan has tricked many so-called NT Churches to teach their members to be obedient to today, because of tithe money. Satan has so deceived some that they rather obey the obsolete covenant, than the everlasting new covenant of Christ, which offers so much more than mere money. But none are as blind as those who simply refuse to see.

WHAT TITHERS DON'T KNOW

Tithers don't know by choosing OT law they have chosen the ministry of death and the ministry of condemnation over the ministries of the Spirit and Righteousness, (2 Cor. 3:7-9). By using the OT law of the tithe instead of the Free- Will -offerings- doctrine Father God established with the first offerings (Ex. 25:2), deceived protithers show greed to be the means by which satan has tricked them into accepting his counterfeit of Christianity. Just like the greed of Adam and Eve, (Gen. 3:6).

How does satan trick people into accepting the OT tithe, and his counterfeit of Christianity? With lying promises of getting them more than they have. The same tactic he uses over and over on the greedy. They believe satan's lie of them getting more with the OT tithe. But in truth the NT is **"a better covenant that was established on better promises" (Heb. 8:6).**

Being able to give financial support for the work of our Lord is a blessing. And it is vitally important that we do so. But equally as important is doing it the right way, according to our Father's instructions. We, the heirs of God with Christ Jesus (Gal. 4:7), as Father has planned (Dan. 7:27) are now being taught to live by His kingdom virtues and character. This is what Lord Jesus was teaching us with the Beatitudes of the Sermon on the Mount (Matt. 5:1-12). We are being prepared to live and reign with our Lord (Dan. 7:27).

The satanic strategy of tricking people to go backwards by using OT laws is designed to stop people from moving forward in the strength and power of the New Covenant. Because the saints of the New Covenant receive Holy Spirit power satan is trying to keep all people away from the New Covenant.

NT TITHE?

When our Lord established the New Covenant, it was for change, it is **"not according to the covenant that I made with their fathers" (Heb. 8:9).** That old covenant of law, the Mosaic covenant, which contained the system of the tithe failed. It failed **"because they did not continue in My covenant, and I disregarded them, says the Lord" (Heb. 8:9).** But the New Covenant is the everlasting covenant with new ways of doing things. God given better ways of doing things.

Many so-called NT Churches today, deceived by satanic lies, with the need or greed for money, are saying no to Father God's new ways of doing things. When it comes to money, they refuse to acknowledge the fact that Father God only accepts what is voluntarily given from the heart (Ex. 25:2). And as a result, they are creating their own downfall. Look around you and you will see tithing churches falling to the ground.

In some tithing churches there remains a faithful few who can't understand why their church is falling apart. Because these faithful ones were faithful to religious tradition, not the Word of God, they are lost in mind and spirit. They remember when there were many people and much money. They were having such a good time doing what they wanted to do, the way they wanted to do it. This went on for so long that they just knew they were doing things right. Then slowly things began to change, the big crowds dwindled to just a few. The money dried up like water in the dessert after a rain. Tradition told them they could use the OT tithe law. But it didn't tell them that doing so places them **"under the curse" (Gal. 3:10).** The bible told them, but they ignored truth, not tradition.

WHAT TITHERS DON'T KNOW

They had learned nothing from the bible about the Amorites whom Father had given four hundred years to straighten up and come back to Him, (Gen. 15:13,16). Four hundred years later they still refused to turn from idol gods and come back to their loving Father. Their whole world fell apart. The tithing churches of today that are falling apart have learned nothing from all those who died in the wilderness. They too wanted to do things their way, instead of God's way.

Tithing churches, deceived by satan and determined to do things other than God's way have Adam and Eve as an example. They had been given the dominion of the whole world (Gen. 1:26) but lost it believing satan's lies of them getting more. Just as tithers do today. Are these things tithers don't know, or things they just don't care about?

If a church uses NT doctrine in everything except matters of money, and it refuses to teach Father God's doctrine of Free- Will-Offerings only (Ex. 25:2), (Ex. 35:5), (Lev. 1:3), (2 Cor. 8:8), (2 Cor. 7:9) etc. And instead teach and preach the OT doctrine of the tithe, is it a NT Church? No. Father God gave the NT Church explicit doctrine and instructions. All are recorded in the scriptures of the NT. It is the following of Father's instructions, the doctrine of the New Covenant, that make a church a NT Church. All others are disobedient impostors.

Father does not accept disobedience, satan does. But for those hearts true to NT doctrine and voluntarily give, **"God is able to make all grace abound toward you, that you, always having all sufficiency in all things, may have an abundance for every good work" (2 Cor. 8:9).** Tithing is OT law, (Heb. 7:5).

NT TITHE?

"Not that we are sufficient of ourselves to think of anything as being from ourselves, but our sufficiency is from God, who also made us sufficient as ministers of the New Covenant, not of the letter (OT) but of the Spirit (NT), for the letter kills, but the Spirit gives life" (2 Cor. 3:5,6). In this passage the apostle Paul explained to the Corinthian Church that NT ministers were not to minister according to the letter of the law. In the Old Covenant Father God wrote the law in letters on stone tablets. But NT ministers are to minister according to the Spirit of the law. The Holy Spirit reveals that Father God, by His great Spirit, has now written His law in hearts and on minds, (Heb. 8:10). The letter kills because the penalty for breaking the law is death. But the Holy Spirit gives life.

So why do people who say they are NT Christians teach the doctrine of an old obsolete covenant (Heb. 8:13). Why do they risk going to hell for ignoring the price Christ paid to establish a new and better covenant for them? Why do they try to hold on to the doctrine of a covenant that was not theirs? The covenant of the Judaic faith. Why? Because satan has deceived them into placing their satanically inspired bad religious traditions ahead of NT doctrine, for money's sake.

Protithers say they are of God but refuse to do what God says. And they believe satanic lies, like the ones who taught them. Why? Because those under the influence of the father of lies will believe a lie before they will the truth every time. As our Lord said, **"This people honors Me with their lips, but their heart is far from Me. And in vain they worship Me, teaching as doctrines the commandments of men" (Mark 7:6,7).**

WHAT TITHERS DON'T KNOW

The satanic lie that the NT Church is supposed to tithe is believed by many because of the biblical truths once associated with the tithe. For example, it is true that the tithe was once a well-established part of life for the people of God. But that was with a different covenant, a different faith (Judaism), a different dispensation (law), and a different culture.

Another reason why so many believe the NT tithe lie is because so much has been written about the tithe in the OT and many people think the OT and the NT are one. However, although the two together make up the Holy Bible, and although the NT is the fulfillment of the OT, they are two bibles and two very different covenants. And they can only be truly understood as such. As Father said the NT is, **"not according to the covenant that I made with their fathers in the day when I took them by the hand to lead them out of Egypt" (Heb. 8:9).**

A Covenant/Testament is a legally binding contract. The OT was a contract between Father and the ancient Israelites. The NT is a contract between Father and Lord Jesus. It includes all Christians because we are in Christ. **"For as many of you as were baptized into Christ have put on Christ" (Gal. 3:27).**

The new covenant, and therefore the NT Church, has absolutely nothing to do with the OT tithe system. The deceived protithers have swallowed satan's scheme hook, line, and sinker. If the need or greed for money had not blinded them, they could see they are helping satan put their life under OT conditions (Gal. 3:12). Satan can't undo what Christ has done so he's trying to get us to reject Christ's accomplishments by tricking us with his lies, something tithers don't know.

THREE

FINANCING CHRIST'S CHURCH

· · · ·

**"SO LET EACH ONE GIVE as he purposes in his heart, not
grudgingly or of necessity, for God loves a cheerful giver."**
(2 Cor. 9:7)

With various donations: Offerings, Contributions, Gifts, Seed
Plantings, Wills and so many other ways to give financial support in
the NT Church, NT ways of support, was the OT tithe ever needed in
Christ's NT Church? No. Not only is it not needed, but it is completely
out of place. The presence of doctrine from the old covenant in the new
covenant Church is heresy, plain and simple. **"In that He says, "A new
covenant," He has made the first obsolete" (Heb. 8:13).** The use of
obsolete doctrine in the NT Church originated with those who have
intentions of destroying Christ's Church and the saints of God, (Rev.
12:17). Just as they are trying to do today.

The OT system of tithing failed. Why would the Lord want that
old corrupted and failed system in His NT Church? Father God was
quite upset with man's continuing acts of corruption, saying, **"Will a
man rob God? Yet you have robbed Me! But you say, in what way
have we robbed You? In tithes and offerings. You are cursed with a
curse, for you have robbed Me, even this whole nation" (Mal. 3:8).**

The tithe was law under the old covenant only. By reading the NT
you will discover, not only does the NT not use OT law, the tithe or
others, but you will also discover that, **"when**

29

NT TITHE?

the fulness of time had come, God sent forth His Son, born of a woman, born under the law, to redeem those who were under the law, that we might receive the adoption as sons" (Gal. 4:4,5). Because OT law is without faith (Gal. 3:12) it's detrimental to those who wish to be Christian, (Gal. 3:11).

Father gave His NT Church His doctrine of volunteerism. Volunteerism is what Father God required in the OT and in the NT. He is the One true God who does not change (Mal. 3:6). Lord Jesus gave the doctrine of volunteerism to His apostles, who then gave it to the NT Church. To the Galatian church the apostle Paul made it clear, saying, **"But I make known to you, brethren, that the gospel which was preached by me is not according to man. For I neither received it from man, nor was I taught it, but it came through the revelation of Jesus Christ" (Gal. 1:11,12).** Lord Jesus revealed the doctrine of the NT.

True to the revelations Paul received from Lord Jesus he always taught the financing of the NT Church was to be done voluntarily. Before Paul became a Christian, he was a Pharisee. And one of the things the pharisees were known for was their keeping of the law. They were dedicated to the law of the tithe. Lord Jesus made mention of their dedication to tithing saying, **"Woe to you, scribes and Pharisees, hypocrites! For you pay tithe of mint and anise and cumin and have neglected the weightier matters of the law: justice and mercy and faith" (Matt. 23:23).** They were so into tithing that they even paid tithes of the spices they grew in their gardens. They were meticulous in keeping the Mosaic laws and were against Christ because they thought He changed the law, (Matt. 5:17).

FINANCING CHRIST'S CHURCH

However, none of the writings of this former pharisee, when discussing the financing of the NT Church, ever mentions a tithe. Paul was the leader in the efforts to collect funds to support the financially exhausted churches in Jerusalem doing a famine. In demonstration of what Lord Jesus had revealed to him about the financing of the NT Church the apostle made it perfectly clear, saying, **"I speak not by commandment, but I am testing the sincerity of your love by the diligence of others" (2 Cor. 8:8).** Tithing, an OT law, was a commandment. But voluntary giving, like our God, is all about love.

The NT tithe lie, like many others lies used by the enemy are not new. From the very beginning of the Church of Christ the satanic powers of darkness have been using lies, satan's favorite weapon, trying to ruin the Lord's Church. The devil tries to trick people with clever imitations of truth, even imitating the Lord's gospel with his counterfeit of Christianity.

"I marvel that you are turning away so soon from Him who called you in the grace of Christ, to a different gospel, which is not another; but there are some who trouble you and want to pervert the gospel of Christ" (Gal. 1:6,7). Sadly, this perverted counterfeit of Christianity is all some people know. Being blinded by bad religious traditions they can't see the truth.

Satan is always trying to trick the children of God to do anything that will bring the wrath of God down of us. Is he succeeding? No. But when people see so many church buildings falling, they think he is. But were these churches of Christ? Or were they tithing churches with leaders who trusted satan's lie more than God's Word? Ask them, they will tell you.

NT TITHE?

Because of the abuse of the tithe system by a corrupt priesthood Father God brought that system to an end. And because it was Jewish and not Gentile it made an unwanted difference at the time when Father was removing all differences in order to bring Jews and Gentiles together as one, His Church.

Father fired the only ones He had given a command to collect tithes (Heb. 7:5), the Levitical priesthood. **"For the priesthood being changed, of necessity there is also a change of law" (Heb. 7:12).** The Priesthood of Melchizedek with the victorious Lord Jesus now the new High Priest replaced the Levitical priesthood, which like the law of Moses, its tithes, and the entire old covenant of law were only temporary.

"Therefore the law was our tutor to bring us to Christ, that we might be justified by faith. But after faith has come, we are no longer under a tutor" (Gal. 3:24,25). And by using the military of Rome Father shut down the only place He had authorized the collection and storage of tithes, the corrupted Temple in Jerusalem, in 70 A.D. NT tithers wake up!

These things were not done in secret, Father God, speaking through His Prophets, made His intention clear by recording it in both the old and new covenants. **"Behold, the day is coming, says the Lord, when I will make a new covenant with the house of Israel and with the house of Judah-not according to the covenant that I made with their fathers" (Jer. 31:31), (Heb. 8:8,9).** Although the absence of scripture including a tithe in the NT Church is evidence, protithers refuse this truth. Just as satan blinded Adam and Eve with lies of their getting more, he has done the same to tithe lovers.

FINANCING CHRIST'S CHURCH

Father said His New Covenant was not according to the Old Covenant. And yet that same old ten percent tithe law is being taught to those seeking God's truth by those who say they are the ministers of the One who's teachings they are ignoring. These so-called NT Churches must answer some questions for themselves. Are we an obedient church of Christ, depending on Him? Or are we another church of satan pretending to be in Christ? Leading people astray and depending on this world and its money! Do we react to what man says or God's Word?

Satan is using the financing of the church and the OT tithe in his deception because he wants to deceive as many as he can. And the financing of the church includes all members. Have you been deceived by the NT tithe lie? Millions of well-intentioned people have been, including myself. It's a very bad religious tradition we inherited from those who came before us. The apostle Peter mentions **"aimless conduct received by tradition from your fathers" (1 Pet. 1:18).** We must make sure those who come after us cannot say the same.

And thanks be to the living God, our Father, now many churches, with Holy Spirit led bible study, now understand this deception and have done away with that old "you must pay your tithe" mentality. They have learned to be true to their covenant and not the failed covenant of the ancient ones, (Heb. 8:13). Lord Jesus gave His life for our new covenant.

But there are still many liars teaching OT law to the NT Church. Some have long realized satan's deception but the greed that made them liars keep them lying. Leading people astray by lying in church for money leads to eternal death.

NT TITHE?

Are you a tither because someone in your church said you were supposed to tithe? Ask that person to show you from NT scripture where it says the NT Church is supposed to tithe. They will always try to convince you with OT scripture because NT scripture does not say that. When they try to convince you with OT scripture kindly remind them that the NT is the covenant of the NT Church, not the OT. Politely point out to them that the old covenant was replaced by the new covenant more than two thousand years ago as (Heb. 8:13) explains. Which means the OT is no one's covenant now!

Ask the protithers in your church to show you in NT scripture where it is recorded that a NT Church, any NT Church, ever tithed, received tithes, taught tithing, or ever had anything to do with tithing. They can't because it does not exist. Tithing was made law by God, to aid His special people in their reformation from the pagans they had become while in Egypt, to the nation of Priests He called them to be. That's why the tithe is only prominent in OT scripture and makes no connection with the NT Church in NT scripture. The Old Covenant came to its end as a covenant the moment Christ died on the cross and the New Covenant began.

Just as the people of the old covenant, mediated by Moses, received the OT law of Moses, the people of the new covenant, mediated by Christ, received the NT law of Christ, the law of love. In the financing of the NT Church, the law of love, Father's doctrine of volunteerism says, **"let each one give as he purposes in his heart, not grudgingly or of necessity; for God loves a cheerful giver" (2 Cor. 9:7).**

34

FINANCING CHRIST'S CHURCH

Father's plan for the salvation of mankind did not stagnant, nor did it go backwards. The fulfilling work of Christ (Matt. 5:17) moved it forward as planned, from Law to Grace. Because the covenant of the NT Church is a covenant of peace and love every aspect of the Church, especially its financing, is to be done by love, voluntarily. **"God is love" (1 John 4:8).** And everything He does is done in love.

What we see in this new covenant of love is our Father's plan for the renewing of His relationship with His creation. The relationship wrecked by Adam and Eve. Because Lord Jesus paid our sin debt, we can again come close to our creator. Now Father God can deal with us under better conditions, much better conditions than the sin mess we were in. Things were made right because Lord Jesus followed Father's instructions, always doing things His way, (John 5:19). Because of our Lord's love for us, and our love for Him, we too must do things, including the financing of His Church, God's way, (Ex. 25:2).

When you tithe in the NT Church you show your support of and your obedience to an OT law and a three-thousand-year-old failed covenant that once belonged to Judaism. The covenant that became obsolete over two thousand years ago, (Heb. 8:13). When you tithe you fail to support the financing of the NT Church according to NT doctrine. And by operating outside of your covenant you also forfeit the power of the new covenant. Which is exactly what satan wants.

Satan's false teachers have given people the impression it is up to them how they do things in the NT Church. People who believe this don't have a good understanding of what it means

NT TITHE?

to be in covenant. It is Father's job as Sovereign, God, and King to make the rules for His covenant. It is our job as covenant subordinates to do as He says. If a person or a people think they might not want to follow all the covenant's rules, they don't need to be included in the covenant. Because once you have entered the covenant you have agreed to do all that the covenant requires. But if you then decided not to do what you have agreed to do, you then open yourself up to whatever punishment, if any, the covenant may provide.

For those people who have been confused by other voices, the voices of those who have their own agenda. The voices that tell people of another way to do things. Remember, when you must know the absolute truth go to the source of all truth, the Bible. If you are not sure how you should give support for God's work here on earth, research it in the book He wrote for you. In it He tells you what you should know.

The Bible is God's book of instructions and so much more. You don't have to be confused because of what they say, you can rely on what God says. Our heavenly Father, He who does not change (Mal. 3:6) made known to the ancient Israelites His doctrine for accepting offerings. **"From everyone who gives it willingly with his heart you shall take My offering" (Ex, 25:2).** This was His instruction for the offerings for the Tabernacle in the wilderness. And the same was used for the Temple in Jerusalem (Luke 21:1-4). And the instruction for the financing of the NT Church is the same. **"So let each one give as he purposes in his heart" (2 Cor. 9:7).** The NT Church is Father God's family who are voluntarily financing Christ's Church.

36

FOUR
UNTWISTING SCRIPTURE

• • • •

"ALL SCRIPTURE IS GIVEN by inspiration of God, and is profitable for doctrine, for reproof, for correction, for instruction in righteousness, that the man of God may be complete, thoroughly equipped for every good work" (2 Tim. 3:16,17).

In their attempts to convince others to become tithers protithers sometimes use twists of scripture. Some who use these twists of scripture know it's wrong but do it anyway. And there are some who use them thinking it must be alright because they see it being done all the time. And then there are those who accept all religious traditions. These can be made to believe wrong is right and right is wrong. They accept all religious traditions without ever examining them. This is how the NT Church became infected with the NT tithe lie. The early NT Church accepted the new, money as tithe tradition, established by the church of Rome, the church of satan.

Some religious people have accepted more twisted scriptures and bad religious traditions of men than they have the true word of God. Usually, it's because they grew up among people who taught them these things by example. **"Do not be deceived: evil company corrupts good habits" (1 Cor. 15:33).** Satanically inspired bad religious traditions are very evil company. The OT tithe in the NT Church is the bad religious tradition responsible for the collapse of so many congregations today. And many church buildings are falling today because of bad religious traditions established with twisted scriptures.

37

NT TITHE?

Scriptures can be twisted in several different ways. Scripture twisters add words to twist scriptures and they omit words to twist scriptures. But the twist used most by protithers is the misapplication of scriptures. The misapplication of scripture is the intentional misplacement of scripture. To knowingly use the wrong scripture as the right context. The misapplication of scripture and the lack of pertinent information concerning the tithe are the protithers most vital helps in convincing people to became tithers. Along with the person's own desire for Christian fellowship. The reason many people join a church.

Another twist protithers use is to quote OT scriptures as if they were NT scriptures. Malachi (3:10) is a classic example of OT scripture being passed off as NT scripture. I have witnessed protithers misuse and misapplication of (Mal. 3:10) for over half a century, most of my church attending life. The most misused application and misrepresentation of the Word of God in the NT Church is: **"Bring all the tithes into the storehouse, that there may be food in My house, and try Me now in this, says the Lord of Hosts, "If I will not open for you the windows of heaven and pour out for you such blessing that there will not be room enough to receive it" (Mal. 3:10).**

This is quoted each Sunday in so-called NT Churches as if it is NT scripture and NT doctrine. People have been hearing this for so long in these Churches that they think it is NT scripture and NT doctrine. But it is not. It is not NT scripture nor is it NT doctrine. It is OT scripture from the old covenant of law that became obsolete over two thousand years ago, (Heb. 8:13). It was a doctrine of Judaism not Christianity.

UNTWISTING SCRIPTURE

Father God spoke (Mal. 3:10) through His prophet to the people of the old covenant four hundred years before Christ was born in Bethlehem. Over four hundred years before Christianity and the NT Church. The tithe was part of their covenant, (Deut. 14:22-29). To be included in a covenant one would have to be alive to agree to the terms of the covenant when it was made, unless otherwise arranged, (Gen. 17:7). There was no NT Church at the time of the old covenant, so how could the NT Church be charged with doing the OT tithe.

Another method of scripture twisters is to teach both the OT and the NT as if the two were one. Although the NT is the fulfillment of the OT each is a different bible. The OT being the Hebrew Bible and the Old Covenant. And the NT being the Christian Bible, the New and better Covenant, (Heb. 8:6).

Although they are very inner related there are many major differences that reason the two should never be taught as one. And although both are covenants, they are very different covenants. Each must be understood from its own perspective. The first lost its covenant legality, being made null and void because of Israel's unfaithfulness to it (Heb. 8:9,13). The second is the everlasting covenant, the New Testament of Lord Jesus and His NT Church. It is the instruction manual for the saints of the NT Church. To teach the two as one is to invite confusion.

Tithing churches will quote part of (Mal. 3:10) with part of (2 Cor. 9:7) while collecting tithes. **"Bring all the tithes into the storehouse" (Mal. 3:10) "for God loves a cheerful giver" (2 Cor. 9:7).** They combine the two scriptures to make it sound like Malachi was also talking to the NT Church.

39

NT TITHE?

When the prophet Malachi was prophesying, around four hundred B. C., the tithe law of God was a tithe of food. **"And you shall eat before the Lord your God, in the place where He chooses to make His name abide, the tithe of your grain and your new wine and your oil, of the firstborn of your herds and your flocks, that you may learn to fear the Lord your God always" (Deut. 14:23).** Why would anyone seeking food ask it of those who would be born hundreds of years after the one asking was no longer alive? He was in no way asking a nonexistent NT Church to tithe. The NT Church was God's secret in Malachi's lifetime, as (Eph. 3:1-7) explains.

The misapplication of OT doctrine from the book of Malachi into the NT Church is the teaching of both covenants as one. It is the protithers insinuation that since the people of the OT being God's people had to tithe, then the people of the NT, also being God's people should tithe too. Therefore, some see a NT tithe as God's plan. But it's satan's plan. While well intentioned, yet not properly informed, and misled into tithing, which is doing OT law (Gal. 3:12), the tither is exactly where satan wants them to be, outside the new covenant.

"But that no one is justified by the (OT) law in the sight of God is evident, for "the just shall live by faith." Yet the (OT) law is not of faith, but "the man who does them shall live by them" (Gal. 3:11,12). You cannot live by that which is without faith and be a Christian. The Christian life is a life of faith. Faith is the very essence of our connection to the living God. **"But without faith it is impossible to please Him" (Heb. 11:6).** The things we live by reveal whose we are.

40

UNTWISTING SCRIPTURE

I tithed for many years growing up in my home church. I grew up listening to twisted scriptures and following along in the satanically inspired bad religious traditions of men. Satan's counterfeit of Christianity was what I was taught. My parents, not knowing the truth themselves, made my siblings and I participate. I thought the counterfeit I was being taught was the real thing. Until I encountered Holy Spirit led bible study. Then I began to see things I had not seen before. I began to see things in the Word of God that were so different from what I had been taught in church. The Spirit of truth and the Word of God enlightened both my mind and my heart.

It is sad when you think about it. How people who read the bible will still believe the twists protithers do to scriptures. Twists that tell them they must do what other people were told to do in the covenant those other people rejected three thousand years ago. And at the same time, reading their bibles, they refuse to believe their own covenant that plainly states: **"But now He (Lord Jesus) has obtained a more excellent ministry, inasmuch as He is also Mediator of a better covenant, which was established on better promises" (Heb. 8:6).**

You cannot live by OT law (Gal. 3:12) and have NT faith. By doing the OT law of the tithe you have rejected the New Covenant and the better laws Christ died to establish for you. Repent! Our Father is ever willing to lovingly forgive. Learn to live by the doctrines of your own covenant. Not the doctrine of an obsolete covenant (Heb 8:13), that once belonged to a different faith (Judaism), thousands of years ago. Why would anyone prefer that old, inferior, God rejected, obsolete covenant?

NT TITHE?

There is only one reason why people use the doctrine of the God rejected covenant (Heb. 8:8,9), instead of the doctrine of the God blessed covenant (Heb. 8:10-12). Because they have been deceived through bad religious traditions like scripture twisting. Some people have been so deceived by scripture twisting and other satanic tricks that they overlook the obvious and fail to recognize simple facts. For example, the fact that the NT Church's foundation is the new and better covenant. Therefore, it does not need to go backwards to a rejected covenant for instructions on financially supporting itself. The bible reveals the tithe system failed in the OT, (Mal. 3:8,9).

And now let's take a closer look at (Mal. 3:10), the passage of scripture that has been twisted the most to support the protithers claim that the NT Church should tithe. The main reason why it has been used most is because it says, **"Bring all the tithe into the storehouse"** **(Mal. 3:10).** If other scriptures said this, they would be used just as much. We must remember no single verse of scripture establishes a doctrine. And the fact (Mal. 3:10) is quoted every Sunday by those who don't know what they are doing surely does not make it NT doctrine.

That this OT scripture is quoted in churches every Sunday shows protithers twisting it from OT to NT scripture. It is a necessary twist for them to get people to think its NT scripture, because the scriptures of the NT make no connection of the NT Church and a tithe. NT scripture says we are not to give **"of necessity"** **(2 Cor. 9:7),** which means when being compelled to give, giving because some say you must. The tithe, an OT law, compelled all under the law to give, (Heb. 7:5).

42

UNTWISTING SCRIPTURE

Malachi (3:10) continues by saying: **"That there may be food in My house"** But in their tithing no one obeys the law of God, which was a law for food. Instead, they tithe money, the change made by the satanic church of Rome. And with the encouragement of protithers the people who are not supposed to tithe, disobey their voluntary offerings doctrine, ignore God's NT law, and accept these illegal twists of scripture made by the powers of darkness. Ignoring how NT scripture said for the NT Church to give, over and over, Sunday after Sunday.

The powers of darkness with satan's spirit of evil, the major contributors of scripture twisting, has many modern twisters in the church today. And they are as effective as twisters of old. I was watching TV as a protithe televangelist was preaching from the seventh chapter of Hebrews to his church. This struck me as very strange because the seventh chapter of Hebrews contains the facts that disprove the NT tithe lie.

The seventh chapter of Hebrews states only the Levitical Priesthood was given God's **"commandment to receive tithes"** (**Heb. 7:5**). And that these tithes were collected **"according to the law"** (**Heb. 7:5**). It also states the tithes were to be collected only **"from their brethren",** the people who like themselves came **"from the loins of Abraham"** (**Heb. 7:5**).

But with all this evidence against a NT tithe, when he got to verse eight where it continues to speak of the Levitical priesthood saying, **"Here mortal men receive tithes"** (**Heb. 7:8**) this scripture twister said, "There it is, you see it for yourself, the bible says mortal men here are to receive the tithes. And like a house full of bobbing head dolls, they all agreed to that lie.

NT TITHE?

Father God gave the commandment to receive tithes to His priesthood only, (Heb. 7:5). It is not recorded anywhere in NT scripture that a NT Church ever tithed. But in the early fourth century A. D. when satan established his church, the church of Rome, in order to make his scheme look legitimate he put priests in his fake NT Church. His church of Rome reintroduced a tithe, not of food but money. And by paying his priests with tithe money collected in his church the door was opened for other churches to do the same. Smuggling OT law into the NT Church. Where it remains among those greedy and blind.

God's commandment to the Levitical Priesthood was that they receive tithes from their brethren only, from those who like themselves came from **"the loins of Abraham" (Heb. 7:5).** But the church of satan collects tithes from all they can convince to pay tithes. Twisters have so twisted scripture that those who don't understand what scripture says are doing what it says not to do, thinking they are blessed for doing it.

God's Word says, **"So let each one give as he purposes in his heart, not grudgingly or of necessity; for God loves a cheerful giver" (2 Cor. 9:7).** Here the Word of God clearly speaks of His doctrine of volunteerism. Where every person gives what they want to give from their heart. Not what someone said they must give. That's not voluntary, not coming from one's own heart. And it says we are not to give grudgingly, when not able to make up our mind to give or not to give. Nor are we to give of necessity. Giving because we feel we must. To give of necessity, not because we want to, but because we feel we must, is not giving voluntarily from the heart.

44

UNTWISTING SCRIPTURE

Remember the tithe was OT law and there is nothing that makes you feel you must do something more than a law. With His doctrine of volunteerism, for both the Old and New Testaments, Father is saying He wants us to support Him the same way He supports us, **"For God so loved that He gave" (John 3:16), and "as He is, so are we in this world" (1 John 4:17).**

But protithers have twisted the Word of God with misapplications of scripture like (Mal. 3:10) which has NT people doing what God said for them not to do, giving of necessity, and has convinced many they will be greatly blessed because of it. But this satanic lie is a trick to get you to continually do OT law, which disqualifies you from being a Christian and having NT Holy Spirit power. **"But that no one is justified by the (OT) law in the sight of God is evident, for "the just shall live by faith." Yet the (OT) law is not of faith, but "the man who does them shall live by them" (Gal. 3:11,12).**

By the power of Father God Lord Jesus was brought back from death. This power is what satan fears most. If he can stop you from becoming a Christian, he can stop you from having this power. He will steal, kill, destroy, and do anything he can to stop you from being in Christ. He has long recognized greed as one of man's worse weaknesses. And he continues to use the same old tactic of offering man more to trick him into doing things satan's way. Even to defy the new covenant.

To be able to effectively fight against satan's evil we must stay prepared for daily spiritual warfare. We must not only walk in the Spirit but also in the knowledge of God's Word, which enables us to untwist twisted scriptures.

FIVE

WHOSE CHURCH?

••••

"AND HE PUT ALL THINGS under His (Christ) feet, and gave Him to be head over all things to the church, which is His body, the fullness of Him who fills all in all" (Eph. 1:22)

Despite Father God's declaration that the New Covenant is not according to the Old Covenant (Jer. 31:31), (Heb. 8:9) there are some who have been so deceived by satan that they are determined to have the OT tithe in the NT Church anyway. Satan has fooled them into thinking they can take in more funds by using the OT tithe, which failed in the old covenant, (Mal. 3:8,9) than they can with new covenant doctrine, the **"better covenant, which was established on better promises" (Heb. 8:6).** Because of satanic influence some church leaders act like they know more about God's Church than He does.

Satan's success has come by tricking people into believing the tithe is NT doctrine, but its OT law, (Deut. 14:22-29). And getting the acceptance of this lie to become religious tradition was started hundreds of years ago in satan's church of Rome. It was in satan's church, with satan's false prophets, and satan's counterfeit of Christianity that the tithe was changed from food to money in order to influence man by his greed. And it still works in many so-called NT Churches today.

Whose church do the protithers think it is? Who are these people who think they can do whatever they want to do? People who have no respect for what God said (John 7:16). Are these just misguided souls, victims of man's religion?

47

ERRY CLEVELAND

NT TITHE?

By their refusal to use the God given doctrine of the NT Church in matters of finance, and teach others to do the same, they identify themselves, **"by their fruits you will know them"** (Matt. 7:20). These are the children of the evil one, walking in the footsteps of their father. Always trying to challenge the authority of the living God. These seeds of satan, like their father, always try to lead the children of God astray with their lies.

They are in the church for many reasons but to help save the lost is not one of them. They come to exhibit their talents, to gather a following for themselves. They come for prestige, to see, and to be seen. And pretend to love the one whose doctrine they ignore. And instead of helping save the lost, many take advantage of the lost, so they can save their money.

When Lord Jesus said, **"on this rock I will build My church, and the gates of Hades shall not prevail against it"** (Matt. 16:18) were these people the gates He had in mind? People who don't seem to understand whose church it is. They try to control the Lord's church as if He, by His great Spirit, was not there. Just as they do in those pretend churches where His Holy Spirit is not. The Diotrephes' of today, (1 John 1:9,10).

Let's take a closer look at what our Lord was saying, **"on this rock I will build My church, and the gates of Hades will not prevail against it"** (Matt. (16:18). The gates represent the authority and power that controls the entrance and exits of the gates. The gates of Hades therefore represent the power and authority of death, which is in opposition of the Lord of the NT Church who came to abolish death, (2 Tim. 1:10). Our Lord put death to death by His victorious resurrection.

8

WHOSE CHURCH?

The word prevail means to overpower, to take control of by a superior strength. Lord Jesus says death, the power and authority of Hades, will never be able to take control of His Church. Because only the Holy Trinity has power and authority in the house of the living God. **"And He (Father God) put all things under His (Lord Jesus) feet, and gave Him to be head over all things to the church, which is His body, the fullness of Him who fills all in all" (Eph. 1:22).**

If it truly is a church of God, and not just a pretender, death will not be able to prevail. Because the God of the NT Church does not just have power, He is the power, the Almighty power. And there is no power that can compare with Him, the creator of heaven and earth. He who is the giver of power.

Consider the group that say they are a NT Church but will not teach the voluntary doctrine of the NT Church. NT doctrine like **"So let each one give as he purposes in his heart" (2 Cor. 9:7).** Have you ever heard them say anything like that? They cling to the devil's doctrine of "get all you can every time". Whose church would you say that is, Christ's or satan's. Can it be Christ's Church that reject His doctrine and use satan's?

What about the groups that have all kinds of programs and special events where members are told to give a certain amount? Do they have all these special events to raise money because they are always in need? Or because greed never gets enough? They tell people if they give, **"God will supply all your need" (Phil. 4:19)** but all their need is never supplied. They always need more, they say. Whose church do you say it is? Is this God's Church or a group of people pretending to be?

NT TITHE?

How can they say they are a church of God when they ignore the doctrines of God, having replaced them with the religious traditions of men? When you willingly ignore the Word of God you are willingly ignoring God. **"In the beginning was the word, and the word was with God, and the word was God" (John 1:1).** NT tithing is a deception from satan's church of Rome, adopted by others. Voluntary offerings only is the God given doctrine for both covenants (Ex. 25:2), (1 Cor. 8:8).

The tithe was something completely different. It was not an offering, as said by those who **"want to pervert the gospel of Christ" (Gal. 1:7).** The tithe was God's portion of the harvests which He used to feed His Priesthood and help those in need. **"You shall truly tithe all the increase of your grain that the field produces year by year" (Deut. 14:22). "And all the tithe of the land, whether of the seed of the land or of the fruit of the tree, is the Lord's. It is holy to the Lord. If a man wants at all to redeem any of his tithe, he shall add one-fifth to it. And concerning the tithe of the herd or the flock, of whatever passes under the rod, the tenth one shall be holy to the Lord" (Lev. 27:30-32).** The tithe was not what man gave God, it was what God gave man, (Deut. 14:23-29), (Num. 18:21).

The Lord could not depend on Israel, when worshiping other gods, to feed His priesthood nor the widows, orphans and strangers among them. Father kept ten percent of all harvests so He, through His priesthood, could do it Himself. The people were not paying tithes, although that is what they called it. They were giving God what belonged to Him. The tithe was not an offering to God. The tithe was what God gave to people.

50

WHOSE CHURCH?

The religious traditionalists are not all that concerned with the truth of God's word. They teach the old covenant's law of the tithe in the Church because it is tradition. They don't know the tradition was started in satan's church with the intention of doing Christ's Church much harm. On those who continue in this bad religious tradition by accepting satan's lies about them getting more, the gates of Hades have already prevailed, not being a true church of Christ.

Are you one whom they have involved in this financial rebellion against the Free- Will- doctrine of God? **"But this I say: He who sows sparingly will also reap sparingly, and he who sows bountifully will also reap bountifully"** (2 Cor. 9:6). **"Then the people rejoiced, for they had offered willingly, because with a loyal heart they had offered willingly to the Lord"** (1 Chr. 29:9). As these examples from both testaments explain, Father's doctrine for accepting offerings have always been voluntary. Man will accept any offering anyway you give it. But God only accepts and blesses offerings given the right way.

If you continue to go along with these bad religious traditions, making offerings man's way instead of God's way, you are as guilty as they are. And you are helping the powers of darkness to rob you! The lack of covenant obedience makes a lack of covenant blessings. Your lack of God's blessings makes satan rejoice. **"The thief does not come except to steal, and to kill, and to destroy. I have come that they may have life, and that they may have it more abundantly"** (John 10:10). If you use any OT law, that places you under OT law (Gal. 3:12). That disqualifies you for the abundant life of the New Covenant.

51

NT TITHE?

In some of the groups that call themselves a NT Church deception is the rule, not the exception. They use the Word of God as blinders to prevent people from seeing the deceptions. However, their use of lies, their twisting of scriptures, and requests for more and more money will eventually reveal to all who are not spiritually unconscious exactly whose church it is.

Our Lord has instructed us to **"Beware of false prophets, who come to you in sheep's clothing, but inwardly they are ravenous wolves. You will know them by their fruits"** (Matt. 7:15,16). The church of Christ or the church of satan, which are you a member of? What does being a member of Christ's Church really mean? It means **"that you are the Temple of God and that the Spirit of God dwells in you?"** (1 Cor. 3:16).

There are many who say they are members of Christ's Church, but don't take the Word of God seriously. They always have time to talk on the phone, but never enough time to talk to God. They spend hours each day on computers but have never tried to compute what God's love should mean to them or what their love would mean to God. They have unlimited time for TV, to party and play games. But only a minute or two, if any, to pray. Are these really members of Christ's Church?

Protithers claim to be members of Christ's NT Church and yet teach the OT tithe doctrine from a covenant that has been obsolete (Heb. 8:13) for over two thousand years. The doctrine not of the Christian covenant, but the doctrine of the Judaic covenant. You can't always rely on what people say. It is imperative that you learn the Bible for yourself. If not, you will never be able to know whose church you are in.

WHOSE CHURCH?

"Give, and it will be given to you; good measure, pressed down, shaken together, and running over will be put into your bosom. For with the same measure that you use, it will be measured back to you" (Luke 6:38). "He who sows sparingly will also reap sparingly, and he who sows bountifully will also reap bountifully" (2 Cor. 9:6). "But when you do a charitable deed, do not let your left hand know what your right hand is doing, that your charitable deed may be in secret; and your Father who sees in secret will Himself reward you openly" (Matt. 6:3,4). Like these, all NT doctrine of financial support are voluntary, giving as God gives (John 3:16).

Under the old Judaic covenant tithe law made the Israelites give Father His ten percent of all harvests. But with the new covenant of peace, "He who did not spare His own Son, but delivered Him up for us all, how shall He not with Him also freely give us all things?" (Rom. 8:32). By tricking the NT Church to do OT law, instead of NT law, satan is trying to make himself look stronger while making Father God look weak. He is always trying to show himself to be a better god than our heavenly Father. That's why he started a rebellion in heaven.

The use of OT doctrine in the NT Church is dangerous. Not only will the use of obsolete doctrine lead those who use them in the wrong direction, but the longer people believe in them the harder it is for them to come to the knowledge of the truth. If you are one of the many who have been tricked into believing the faithless OT tithe (Gal. 3:12) belongs in the NT Church you have been setup to reject the New Covenant in the satanic hope of your eternal destruction (Heb. 10:28,29).

NT TITHE?

Some who call themselves Christians are working with satan and don't even know it. They have been so deceived that they are passing on to others satan's deceptions, thinking they are doing what's right, when it's so dangerously wrong. Some don't know and others don't care what doing OT law does to those who do them in this dispensation of God's grace. A time of loving reconciliation, not a time of lawful retribution.

The bible says, **"You have been estranged from Christ, you who attempt to be justified by law; you have fallen from grace"** (Gal. 4:5). And that you are to, **"Stand fast therefore in the liberty by which Christ has made us free, and do not be entangled again with a yoke of bondage. Indeed I, Paul, say to you that if you become circumcised (the first OT law) Christ will profit you nothing"** (Gal. 5:2). That Christ will profit the NT Church nothing if it uses OT law is satan's purpose for sneaking every OT law he can into the NT Church. But the tithe law is the pinnacle of his success because of man's great weakness, greed. Satan uses this weakness in his tactics over and over. And it works today as well as it ever did.

I know the truth about the fake NT tithe will make many people angry. It certainly made me angry when it was revealed to me that it is a satanic lie and a bad religious tradition. And it makes you even more angry when you realize this has been robbing you of your God given blessings for so long. Because Father does not bless disobedience. And that you have been paying for this yourself is something not easy to forget. If you must blame someone, blame the right one, blame yourself for doing what man said, instead of what God said.

WHOSE CHURCH?

The fake NT tithe is one of satan's most cleverly disguised tricks. The work of the one who **"deceives the whole world"** (Rev. 12:9). It's one of his master lies. But as Lord Jesus has said, **"the truth will make you free" (John 8:32).** The Word of God is the foundation of wisdom, knowledge, and truth. Therefore, you must **"be diligent to present yourself approved to God, a worker who does not need to be ashamed, rightly dividing the word of truth" (2 Tim. 2:15).**

Many have been tithing most of their life. I did for over thirty years. Some of these when confronted with the truth of this fake will reject it. They are too ashamed to admit that they, Christians, have been so wrong for so long. Others say they can't see how something that's been going on in their church for so long could be a trick of the devil. That's because they could not see whose church it was, Christ's or satan's.

To these people I ask this question. Have you never heard of the Doctrine of Indulgence? Look it up. This was another trick from the church of satan. It was as sinister as the fake NT tithe. It was introduced to the world by the Popes of the satanic church of Rome. It was the sale of the forgiveness of sin and the remission of purgatorial punishments for money.

By the time it was finally exposed to the world as the satanic lie it was, some Popes had amassed more wealth than some Kings. The lie from satan's false church that Father God had given the Popes authority to forgive sins for money to build Saint Peter's Cathedral lasted for over four hundred years. The fake Church of Rome also embraced the ancient pagan spring festival known as Easter and smuggled it into Christ's Church.

NT TITHE?

The great reformer Martin Luther and the other saints who worked with him to bring this farce to light discovered, as I have, that some of the traditions we were taught did not come from the Church of Christ, but from the church of satan.

Our heavenly Father not only forgives, but He also lovingly understands. My parents started me tithing. They thought they were teaching me the right thing to do. It was their understanding that if you worked and were a member of the church you were supposed to tithe. This is what they had received, and this is what they passed on to me. But they, like millions of others, were merely following the religious traditions of men. Never knowing who started the tradition or why, because it became church tradition it continued. That's the way traditions work and that's why satan uses traditions to lead God's people astray. Religious tradition has become a satanic weapon.

The bible says, **"For God is not the author of confusion but of peace, as in all the churches of the saints"** (1 Cor. 14:33). But If Father said, **"You shall truly tithe all the increase of your grain that the field produces year by year"** (Deut. 14:22). Then say to the same people, **"Whoever is of a willing heart, let him bring it"** (Ex. 35:5) wouldn't that be confusion? No. What must be understood is the fact that the OT tithe was not an offering but a law, (Lev. 27:30). The people of the OT only had a law that made them give God His ten percent of all harvests. But both covenants gave the freedom to give as offerings whatever was in the heart. To have both apply to the NT Church is a bad religious tradition, inspired by satan, that is never recognized by those who don't know whose church they're in.

56

SIX
GOD OF LAW

• • • •

"FOR ASSUREDLY, I SAY to you, till heaven and earth pass away, one jot or one tittle will by no means pass from the law till all is fulfilled" (Matt. 5:18).

Our heavenly Father is the God of law. Those who seek to be Christian, who wish to be in the family of the living God must study to learn as much as one can about the God of law and about the laws of God. We need to understand how the laws of God pertain to us today. We must understand that the laws of God came to us via His chain of command.

We must learn the laws of God because of our enemies, spiritual hosts of wickedness. Our enemies design their tricks around the laws of God. They use what they know about God's laws and what people don't know to deceive and confuse. This is exactly what was done to bring the OT tithe law into the NT Church. What you don't know about God's laws can and will be used against you in Spiritual warfare.

When the bible says "the law" it is referring to the law of the OT, the Mosaic law, also known as the Mosaic covenant. It was known as "the law" because for 1500 years it was the only law Israel ever had. It was "the law" until the coming of Christ, who gave the world His NT law, also known as the law of Love.

The bible speaks of the law of the OT and the law of the NT, both are the laws of God. OT law is called the law of Moses because he mediated the Old Covenant. NT law is called the law of Love and of Christ because He mediated the New Covenant.

57

NT TITHE?

But what is a Covenant? And why are they so important? A Covenant and a Testament are the same thing, contracts that are legally binding according to the laws of God. Our heavenly Father is not only The God, The Creator, and The Sovereign of the universe, but He is also The Sovereign Judge of creation. Because He is the righteous judge, He conducts all His affairs in a just and judicious manner. He is the covenant making and covenant keeping God. Creator of heaven and earth.

Because He is the Lord God, Sovereign Creator, Judge and King, He is the one who makes the rules for His Covenants. Mankind can only accept or reject being in covenant with Father God. From the Edenic covenant of Adam and Eve to today's New Covenant, Father always deals with man in ways that are just, legally binding, and according to covenant.

The law of God was not the same in the old and new covenants, there was a difference. It was not that the law said something in one covenant that it said differently in the other covenant. The difference was in the developmental stages of the law. Unlike the people of the new covenant who received the law fulfilled by Christ, the people of the old covenant received the law in its elemental phase, new to them, written in letters on stone tablets. But having lived in Egypt for over four hundred years they only knew Egyptian Hieroglyphics.

Father God gave His people OT law to temporarily aid them in their state of arrested development. **"It (OT law) was added because of transgressions, till the Seed (Christ) should come to whom the promise was made" (Gal. 3:19).** The penalty for breaking the law, death, taught the seriousness of sin.

GOD OF LAW

A provision of OT law is, **"the man who does them shall live by them"** (Gal. 3:12). Father made this provision of the law to keep those under the law moving in the right direction, away from idolatry. This helped the people to stop going back and forth from God's law to pagan rites. God's laws of the OT were good for OT people. OT law served them much better than their living with pagan rites. But all changed with the NT.

When God's program changed, elevated by the coming of the Messiah and a New Covenant that included the fulfillment of OT laws, man's relationship with the laws of God changed also. OT law that was without faith (Matt. 5:17) was fulfilled to NT law, the law of Christ, the law of love. Which is how Lord Jesus**, "redeemed those who were under the (OT) law, that we might receive the adoption as sons"** (Gal. 4:4,5). Because OT law is without faith those under OT law cannot be adopted into the family of God. The reason why satan has tried to sneak every OT law he could, like the tithe, into the NT Church.

No matter which OT law you have been tricked into doing, tithing, the Kosher food laws, the Levirate marriage law, circumcision or any other OT law, the result is the same. **"But that no one is justified by the (OT) law in the sight of God is evident, for "the just shall live by faith"** (Gal. 3:11).

Although the use of OT law is a downfall for the people of the NT Church, it was good for the people of the OT. The provision that, **"the man who does them shall live by them"** (Gal. 3:12) was intended to keep the people of the OT doing OT law until Christ and faith in Him had been established. **"Therefore, the law was our tutor to bring us to Christ"** (Gal. 3:24).

NT TITHE

Faith in Christ could not be established until He had come into the world and accomplished those things that would give people faith in Him. He came into the world and lived a sinless life. He came and taught man by example the true ways of God, the ways God had intended for mankind to live. To show the power of faith He did many miracles. And by voluntarily giving His life on a cross He paid mankind's sin debt, taking on Himself the sin of the world, and after three days walked out of the grave. Establishing faith in Himself and His New Covenant.

Even though Christ has come into the world and has done those things that established faith in Him, giving His life to redeem the world from faithless OT law with a new covenant and NT law. And even after all He suffered to give the world a **"better covenant that was established on better promises" (Heb. 8:6)**, there are still people who allow themselves to fall for satan's lies that the OT tithe is better than the doctrine of the NT. Despite the fact the tithe failed in the OT, (Mal. 3:8).

But satan's people will believe a lie before they will the truth because they don't have the spirit of truth in them, (John 14:17). If the people who tithe understood what they were doing, they would never do it. But we have an enemy who does understand this and not only this, but he understands man. Having dealt with mankind for so long satan knows man's strengths and weaknesses. This is the one who tricked Adam and Eve out of the world dominion Father God gave them. All satan gave for it was lies. Today he still uses lies to make people think it's alright to break God's law. God's law says do not murder, satan's lies say abortion is alright.

60

GOD OF LAW

But there came a time when a new development called for a readjustment of God's law. Only the God of law Himself can change or make readjustments to His law. Which He has done more than once to make things better. Because He is Sovereign both the world and the law are His. Others have tried to change God's laws, but the law was not changed by them, only unjustifiably tampered with. He is the only Sovereign.

With the Lord God's rescue of ancient Israel, after hundreds of years of slavery in Egypt, came the realization that they had become as pagan as the nations around them. The people of God had become the people of gods. There were only two things needed to be done. God's chosen people had to be educated out of their paganism and re-educated into the will and ways of the one true God, the God of their forefathers.

Their idolatrous ways had to go so the light and love of God would have room to grow in their hearts. Israel had to go to school and be taught anew what they had forgotten, the ways of their fathers Abraham, Isaac, and Jacob. But how do you get over a million people together for school and where? And how would you feed over a million people in school? Being the God of law Father naturally decided to do this by law. What was a voluntary tithe Father made into an OT law (Deut. 14:23-29). Assuring attendance and food for all.

Ancient Israel went into Egypt seeking food because of a great famine. To their amazement they were reunited with Joseph, Egypt's Prime Minister, national hero, and favorite long-lost son of their father Jacob. They were welcomed and given the respect due the family of the nation's hero.

NT TITHE?

But after Joseph died and a new Pharaoh who did not know Joseph came to the throne his people were enslaved because the Egyptians feared their vast multitudes. The Egyptians, like all their neighbor nations were pagans, people who worshiped many gods. The 430 years ancient Israel was in Egypt made them pagans also. Israel worshiped all the gods of the other pagans. And in so doing they lost the knowledge of and dedication to the one true God. They had begun to see all gods the same, even their forefather's God of law.

This was totally unacceptable to Father God. This was altogether out of line with His plans for His chosen people and the world. He had revealed to Abraham, their patriarch, that after 400 years He would bring Abraham's family, then a very numerous people, back to the land He had given them by law of covenant. They had been chosen by God to be unto Him a special people. He, as their God, had given them a special place in His plans for the salvation of mankind.

But the nation Israel was, when first freed, was not the nation that could accomplish or even be interested in Father's plans for them. Israel would have to become a different nation; they would have to learn to be like their forefathers. What was at stake was no less than the salvation of mankind.

Father God's plan called for a nation of holy people, a nation of priests, totally devoted to the one true God. A people who would be an example worthy of being copied by the many lost nations of the world. Israel would have to be a special people to be the people of the special God. The God of law would teach them to be a people of the law and love.

GOD OF LAW

Ancient Israel had become a very sinful people, unlike their patriarchs. Over four hundred years in Egypt had left its mark. To accomplish His plan Father would have to teach them to embrace righteousness. Being the great Judge of the world Father would do this within the confines of law. And being one who always does first things first, since sinful Israel was living their lives without regard of morals, the first thing Father did was to give them His moral laws, His eternal moral code, His Ten Commandments. A major step in the right direction.

In Exodus chapter twenty it is recorded how Father God came down on Mt. Sinai and spoke to the children of Israel. They heard the actual voice of the living God as He gave them His Ten Commandments, His moral laws. The importance of His law is seen in the fact that Father did not rely on anyone else to deliver them. That Israel received His laws meant even more because they received them from God Himself.

These ex-slaves were shocked by what they heard. So much so that they didn't want to hear again the voice on the one who had rescued them. **"Then they said to Moses, "You speak with us, and we will hear; but let not God speak with us, lest we die" (Ex. 20:19).** They asked Moses to have God speak to him and then for him to tell them what God said. They were afraid if they heard God's voice again, they would die.

They were very afraid and rightly so, because the very first words they heard Father God speak were a serious indictment against them. What they heard spelled trouble for them. The first words these idol worshipers heard were Father God's number one law. That there be no other gods beside Him.

63

NT TITHE?

Father spoke this to a people who worshiped many gods. They did not want to hear what else He might say. They had witnessed His great power when He rescued them from Egypt. This did not sit well in the minds of people who worshiped gods of heaven and earth. Nor did this sit well with the one who was giving this law to His chosen people, whom He knew had become pagans. This was not only the first hurdle Israel had to cross, but it was also their highest. While Israel or any other nation worships another god, they can never become the nation God called them to be. Total dedication to the one true living God is what makes all God given missions successful. Father said, **"I am the Lord and there is no other" (Isa. 45:18).**

What once was a voluntary tithe (Gen. 14:20), the God of law changed into the law of the tithe (Heb. 7:5). With this law in place Father God began what must have been the greatest re-education project in the world, up to that time. He had over a million people who were key to His plan that didn't know Him, nor who they were supposed to be.

As part of the Deuteronomic Code tithe law stated the tithe had to be eaten before the Lord God, (Deut. 14:23). Which meant all tithers had to come together at a certain place to participate in what was known as the Festival Tithe. **"But you shall seek the place where the Lord your God chooses, out of all your tribes, to put His name for a dwelling place; and there you shall go" (Deut. 12:5).** To do this all had to come to wherever the Ark of the Covenant was. The Ark of the Covenant, also known as the Ark of the Testimony, was the earthly throne of God, where God met with Moses.

64

GOD OF LAW

The Ark was moved from tribal center to tribal center. The people had to take the tithe food to wherever the Ark was because the Ark represented the presence of the invisible God. This is how Father would bring all Israel together and teach them. He made a special rule for those who lived to far to carry the tithe with them. The rule was for them to sell the tithe foods where they lived, take the money with them to the tithe sight and buy whatever they wanted.

"And you shall spend that money for whatever your heart desires: for oxen or sheep, for wine or similar drink, for whatever your heart desires; you shall eat there before the Lord your God, and you shall rejoice, you and your household" (Deut. 14:26). Protithers and religious traditionalists who teach the false NT tithe, teach people they are to give the tithe to them for God. Here we see the true nature of the tithe. We see God giving His tithe (Lev. 27:30) to His people and encouraging them all to rejoice. The God of law is also the God of Love.

This was quite possibly the very first party with a purpose. Father God arranged for all His children to be where His will, His ways and His laws were being taught. His use of the tithe by making it an OT law did exactly as He had planned. This gathering of all the tribes of Israel was unlike any other gathering since they all waved Egypt goodbye. Here they would be taught what they did not know about the God of their forefathers. And they wanted to know more about this great power who pushed Egypt aside like dust. Who made the waters of a sea stand up and bow as the children of Israel past through on dry land? The one who revealed Himself as "I AM".

NT TITHE?

But this gathering was for much more than just school. Father also brought all His chosen ones together to celebrate. This was to be a time of great rejoicing. To celebrate the accomplishments of the many promises Father God made to Israel over many years. It was the perfect way for them to see just who this great God of law really is. And in this exalted atmosphere of joy and love Israel celebrated the God of law.

They celebrated being a free people after hundreds of years as slaves. In this Festival Tithe they were not only here to learn, but also to eat and drink and be merry. The food of the tithe was of major importance. It was the realization of the promised land flowing with milk and honey. God gave them His tithe to enjoy in His presence. Reminding Israel of all His provisions.

The God of law had given His people His moral laws, His Ten Commandments, civic and ritual laws. All these laws were to protect God's people and any other people from falling into paganistic idolatry. However, having God's laws and continuing to live by God's laws are two different things. The peer pressure of the demoralized lifestyle of their neighbors was strong. Baalism, the sexually driven religious system so close to the children of God created a devastating development. Ancient Israel jumped out of the Egyptian frying pan into the Canaanite fire. It would be some time before they came to appreciate the protective power of God's laws.

Today the demonic influence that led Israel away from the protective power of God's laws are at work using an obsolete OT law, the tithe, to do the same to the NT Church. Greed is a tool of satan, learn to trust the doctrine of the God of law.

SEVEN
LACK OF KNOWEDGE

....

"BE DILIGENT TO PRESENT yourself approved to God, a worker who does not need to be ashamed, rightly dividing the word of truth" (2 Tim. 2:15).

Many of the people in Christ's New Covenant Church are being duped into using OT law, obsolete doctrine from an obsolete covenant that once belonged to the people of a different faith, (Heb. 8:8,9). And some NT leaders refuse to teach and enact the Voluntary- Offering- Only doctrine established by Father God, perfectly explained in the very first offerings recorded (Ex. 25:1,2), and acknowledged in the scriptures of both covenants. The Voluntary- Offering- Only doctrine was established by **"He who changes not"** (Mal. 3:6).

Why are so many church leaders ignoring Father God's instructions, and are perfectly willing to teach God's Church whatever they want to teach? There are no simple answers, there are many and they are cloudy. There are however observations that will lead a person seeking the truth in the right direction. If they can recognize these observations.

The inability to recognize these telling observations point to one thing, the lack of biblical knowledge. It's one of the reasons why people allow satan to trick them into using the dead obsolete doctrine (Heb. 8:13) of the old covenant where the doctrine of the new covenant is required, (Heb. 8:6). It's the reason why hospital beds are full of people **"having a form of godliness but denying its power"** (2 Tim. 3:5).

67

NT TITHE?

There are reasons why some people continue to lack bible knowledge. But the lack of bible knowledge is usually the results of a lack of bible study. No matter how much we encourage someone to study God's Word its always up to them. "You can lead a horse to water, but you cannot make it drink." Bible study is one of the most valuable ministers of any church.

The lack of bible knowledge always remains with those who try to understand without the number one ingredient necessary to do so, the Spirit of God. **"But the natural man does not receive the things of the Spirit of God, for they are foolishness to him; nor can he know them, because they are spiritually discerned" (1 Cor. 2:14).** Biblical knowledge comes when the Spirit of God is our guide. **"When He, the spirit of truth has come, He will guide you into all truth" (John 3:6).**

To receive the gift of a portion of God's Spirit you only need to ask Him. He is more than willing to share His Spirit with those who ask in sincerity. To receive of God's Spirit is to be born again. **"That which is born of the flesh is flesh, and that which is born of the Spirit is Spirit" (John 3:6).** We must ask for a portion of His Spirit; He does not force it on anyone because He created us with free will. We were given free will by being created in God's image and likeness, (Gen. 1:26).

Father could have created us so we would never sin or do anything wrong. But that would have made us only programed robots. Which would have defeated His purpose and glorious intentions. Father is creating His forever family. He is creating a family to be part of Him. A loving family worthy of a new heaven and new earth created by the loving Father of all.

68

THE LACK OF KNOWLEDGE

Among other things, Father sent Lord Jesus to be the pattern for His children because **"He is the image of the invisible God"** (Col. **1:15).** Father is creating a family not only to be with Him but to be part of His plans made before the foundation of the earth. **"Then the kingdom and dominion, and the greatness of the kingdoms under the whole heaven, shall be given to the people, the saints of the Most High"** (Dan. 7:27).

To be born of God's Spirit opens our spirit eyes and mind so we can understand the things God wants us to understand. **"Now we have received, not the spirit of the world, but the spirit who is from God, that we might know the things that have been freely given to us by God"** (1 Cor. 2:12). When we receive the Spirit of God that does not instantly give us all we need to end our lack of knowledge. We must still study God's Word. The study of the bible is not just to learn facts. It is the process by which we grow spiritually. Being led by the Spirit of God within us, we are also being spiritually fed by the Word.

People also lack biblical knowledge because they are already filled with another knowledge. The wrong knowledge that comes by having the spirit of satan at work in them. Many have been filled with satanically inspired bad religious traditions like a NT tithe. Instead of believing what God said, it has become their tradition to believe what man said God said.

Many have accepted what man said God said about a NT tithe. Not only did God not say what they claim He said, but in fact God's Word says the opposite. The tithe was an OT law, and OT law has nothing to do with the NT Church. Lord Jesus in giving His life redeemed us from OT law, (Gal. 4:4,5).

69

NT TITHE

NT scripture says, **"So let each one give as he purposes in his heart, not grudgingly or of necessity; for God loves a cheerful giver"** (2 Cor. 9:7). To give of necessity means to give because of constraint, being pressured to do, forced to do. To give because of a law is to give of necessity. **"And indeed those who are the sons of Levi, who receive the priesthood, have a commandment to receive tithes from the people according to the law, that is from their brethren, though they come from the loins of Abraham"** (Heb. 7:5,6). "According to the law".

There is nothing that makes anything more of a necessity than a law that says you must do it. The fact that people in the NT Church give of necessity, even though the NT says not to, is an observation pointing to their lack of knowledge. Instead of them doing what God said, because of their tradition, they are doing what man said God said.

The tithe, a law, was a necessity in the old covenant but not the new covenant. It was a law that said God's covenant people had to give God the ten percent of all harvests that belonged to Him. Father gave the ancient Israelites ninety percent of all harvests, keeping the ten percent for Himself. The law said, **"You shall truly tithe all the increase of your grain that the field produces year by year"** (Deut. 14:22). **"And concerning the tithe of the herd or the flock, of whatever passes under the rod, the tenth one shall be holy to the Lord"** (Lev. 27:32). **"And all the tithe of the land, whether of the seed of the land or of the fruit of the tree, is the Lord's. It is holy to the Lord"** (Lev. 27:30). But nowhere in all of NT scripture is it recorded that a NT Church ever tithed. It was OT law only.

70

THE LACK OF KNOWLEDGE

Because of a lack of bible knowledge and not accepting what the Word of God has said but believing the satanically inspired bad religious traditions of man, many church going people have ignored God's Free- Will- Offerings-Only doctrine. God's Free- Will- Offerings- Only doctrine is prominently revealed in both the old and new covenants. It was established and recorded in the very first offerings. **"From everyone who gives it willingly** (voluntarily) **with his heart you shall take My offering" (Ex. 25:2), from the OT. "So let each one give as he purposes in his heart"** (voluntarily) **(2 Cor. 9:7),** from the NT.

Your blessings do not come because of what man says God said. Your blessings come when you give from your heart, as God said. The blessings of God come upon the obedient not the disobedient. To be obedient you must know what God has said. Notice in both verses above you see the phrase "his heart". In both the Word of God says God accepts offerings from the heart only. The tithe was not an offering but an OT law. Those who tithe in the NT Church greatly display their lack of knowledge by their misuse of Father's instructions.

The dedicated study of God's Word, led by the Spirit of God, has saved many from being wounded by satan's NT tithe lie. Holy Spirit led bible study showed me the danger of the NT tithe lie. To reject Father's Free- Will- Offerings- Only doctrine and accept the OT tithe from the obsolete covenant that once belonged to Judaism (Heb. 8:13) as an offering, is one of the most dangerous things a person can do. To reject the doctrine of the NT is to reject both Lord Jesus and Father God. Which is spiritual suicide (Heb. 10:28,29) and exactly what satan wants.

71

NT TITHE

Because of a lack of knowledge people miss so many of the obvious signs that say stop something is wrong. Things that a true student of the word, one who loves the Word of God can see from afar. My early lack of bible study and being filled with the bad religious traditions of man made me miss all the stop signs that are so obvious to me now. When the Holy Spirit brings you out of the darkness of man's bad religious traditions into the light of God's Word it is wonderfully illuminating.

The first and most obvious sign that it's wrong to use a tithe in the NT Church is the fact we are not instructed to do so anywhere in NT scripture. And when rightly dividing the word, it says not to tithe. Being told to do something NT scripture reveals as never having been done in the NT Church is another obvious stop sign that is never seen by those with so little bible knowledge that they don't know what NT scripture says about the subject. These people are always at the mercy of others.

The very nature of the OT tithe law points to its uselessness in the dispensation of grace. The tithe law was never needed in the NT Church because the reason for the tithe law never existed in the NT Church. The tithe was made law for Israel's re-education, to end their idolatry. The NT Church helps reshape the lives of people once engaged in idolatry, but not with OT laws, with the NT and the love of God through Christ Jesus.

Israel's Festival tithe was very important. After hundreds of years in pagan Egypt the children of Israel had all but forgotten about the God of their forefathers. They had no special concern for one they thought to be just another god. The festival tithe, a time to learn, addressed their lack of knowledge.

THE LACK OF KNOWLEDGE

Israel's once voluntary tithe was made law in order to get all of Israel in one place at the same time to learn. The festival tithe congregation was there so Father could deal with their lack of knowledge. It was of the utmost importance that they receive knowledge of the one true living God. The God who had chosen Israel to be His own people. The festival tithe was the place, the tithe was the food, and the priesthood, the collectors of God's tithe were the people's instructors.

As God's chosen people Israel had been assigned a very important position in Father's plan for the salvation of mankind. The festival tithe brought all Israel together every six months. It became a place of joyful fellowship, being together in thanks and praises to the Lord their God (Deut. 14:21-27). Here they would be taught the values of their fathers, Abraham, Isaac, and Jacob. Here they would learn who God is, and who the children of Israel were supposed to be.

But the festival tithe, like all other tithes, served its purpose under the old covenant. The tithes were not offerings to God, as the enemy would have you think. The tithes were not what man was giving to God, but as the festival tithe shows, the tithes were what God was giving to man (Num. 18:21). The Mosaic covenant came to its end and the covenant of Christ took over. That change did not mean there was to be a compulsory gathering of offerings in the voluntary Church of Christ. To the biblically knowledgeable the OT tithe in the NT Church sticks out like a red head in a house full of blondes. And yet this satanic interference of the voluntary doctrine Father gave to the old and new covenant has continued due to man's greed.

73

NT TITHE?

When people are asked to become tithers there are somethings they are not told. This knowledge is not being withheld from the people on purpose. The person asking them to become tithers don't have this knowledge themselves. If they did, they would not be a tither. The knowledge they lack prevents them from seeing that they are working with satan against themselves. A satanic trick, a NT tithe, was designed around the Word of God and one of man's worse weaknesses, greed.

By the rejection of the God given doctrine of voluntary offerings only (Ex. 35:5), and the acceptance of the satanically inspired bad religious tradition of a NT tithe, satan has tricked many saints into rejecting their own covenant. If you had been **"diligent to present yourself approved to God, a worker who does not need to be ashamed, rightly dividing the word of truth"** (2 Tim. 2:15) you would have known that **"wide is the gate and broad is the way that leads to destruction, and there are many who go in by it"** (Matt. 7:13).

Because of a lack of knowledge some think that although we are in covenant with God, we can still do whatever we want to in the NT Church. To the one who said, "I tithe because that's what my congregation wants to do", I must ask. Are they your Lord? Did your congregation die for you? Can they keep you out of hell? Have they been given all authority?

Because we are in covenant with God, we have agreed to do what He says. Let's not make Him say about us what He said about others, **"My people are destroyed for a lack of knowledge, because you have rejected knowledge, I will reject you from being priest for Me"** (Hosea 4:6), (Rev. 5:10).

EIGHT
THE CURSES OF OT LAW

• • • •

"FOR AS MANY AS ARE of the works of the law are under the curse" (Gal. 3:10). "And indeed those who are the sons of Levi, who receive the priesthood, have a commandment to receive tithes from the people according to the law" (Heb. 7:5).

They were cursed by God. The whole nation. And not just any nation but God's chosen people, Israel, the apple of God's eyes. To the nation through whom He would bring the Messiah into the world God instructed His prophet to say, **"You are cursed with a curse, for you have robbed Me, even this whole nation" (Mal. 3:9).** Why would anyone want to rob God?

They were cursed because of covenant disobedience. They refused to be obedient to the covenant they had agreed to. They could not continue in all things written in the law to do them. And they would not honor their own oath. **"All that the Lord has said we will do, and be obedient" (Ex. 24:7).** What was the object of their disobedience? Old Covenant Law. They stopped doing what the Mosaic law required. They stopped giving the Lord His tithe, they stopped making proper offerings and stopped doing proper sacrifices.

"You offer defiled food on My altar" (Mal. 1:7). "And when you offer the blind as a sacrifice, is it not evil? And when you offer the lame and sick, is it not evil? (Mal. 1:8). "And you bring the stolen, the lame, and the sick; thus you bring an offering! Should I accept this from your hand?" (Mal. 1:13).

75

NT TITHE?

The tithe was the ten percent of all harvested agricultural products that Father God retained for Himself, (Lev. 27:30-32). Offerings were the voluntary gifts the people gave to honor God. Giving Father God His tithes and their offerings showed their appreciation of all Father had done for them. The tithe food was proof that Father God kept His promises. He had promised to free them from slavery and give them a land of their own, a land flowing with milk and honey. And by doing this He proved that everything belonged to Him.

As Israel grew so did the tithes and the laws of the tithes. But the main uses of the system remained, to honor God the great provider by giving Him His portion of the harvest first. Which He gave to feed His priesthood, all those at the festival tithe, widows, strangers, and any of the people in need. For many years the tithe and its laws were respected, and the system worked well. But the increasing misuse and abuse by the priesthood (Mal. 1:7,8) created a time when almost everyone stopped tithing, making offerings and sacrifices. The whole system had been corrupted by the satanic influence of greed.

In the apostate churches of today the circumstances are reversed but the outcome is the same, covenant disobedience. Those who were under the old covenant of law were given the tithe and its laws, but because of the satanic influence of greed in the priesthood people refused to tithe, though it was OT law. People in the apostate churches of today, not given the laws of a tithe, because of the satanic influence of greed, being deceived, tithe anyway. Ignoring the truth that Lord Jesus has redeemed all people from all OT laws, (Gal. 4:4,5).

CURSES OF OT LAW

Those OT tithe laws were given to Israel only. They were given in a different dispensation of time and purpose. For the covenant mediated by Moses, and the covenant mediated by Lord Jesus, Father God established His Free- Will- Offerings-Only doctrine (Ex. 25:2), (Ex. 35:5), (Lev. 1:3). The tithe, not an offering, was something totally different and for totally different purposes. Those who insist on a NT tithe do so because they have been deceived by a bad religious tradition started by the satanic powers of darkness in satan's church of Rome.

For the Church of Christ's first three hundred years there was no mention of a tithe. And the Christian Church had no priests. But in the early fourth century A. D. came satan's church of Rome, complete with the unholy trinity's collection of priests and their resurrected use of the tithe. The tithe system had been decommissioned by Father God with the destruction of the corrupted Jerusalem Temple in 70 A.D. With his false church, false prophets, false priests, and false tithe system, satan established his counterfeit Christianity. Designed so much like true Christianity that only the blood bought, Word washed, born again, see the difference.

Protithers are so wrapped up in the idea of more money that they don't see the devil gladly paying them to cut their own throat. To claim you are a Christian but teach and preach the doctrine of the God rejected old covenant (Heb. 8:13), twisted and presented as NT doctrine, is exactly what you are doing, cutting your own throat. You may be able to use the NT tithe lie to get money, but what about the curse (Gal. 3:10)? And what about the judgement of God (Heb. 10: 28-30)?

NT TITHE?

Protithers don't tell people the tithe is OT law. Or that OT law has nothing to do with faith. They don't explain that God's law (Gal. 3:12) says whoever does OT law shall live by OT law. So, when a person becomes a tither, they are living by faithless OT law. Which means, because their life is being lived in faithlessness they cannot be justified (declared righteous) by God, (Gal. 3:11). Only those who live by faith can be justified (imputed the righteousness of Christ).

Satan, who has deceived protithers and religious traditionalists into working with him, whether they know it or not, is a supreme trickster and the world's biggest liar. He has smuggled not only the OT tithe, but every OT law he could into the NT Church. His most successful lie has been a NT tithe because his false church resurrected the tithe and changed it to money.

Protithers have led many of the people they love in the wrong direction by telling them they have to tithe. Many protithers teach this because they believe this themselves. It is satanic deception by use of religious tradition. Because so many people have taken part in NT tithing for so long it has been implanted into their minds as something they know for sure to be real, even though it's not. We must realize biblical knowledge is the Word of God only, not the traditions of man. Not only does NT scripture make no connection of a tithe and the NT Church, but NT scripture says not to tithe when it says not to give **"of necessity (2 Cor. 9:7)**. The Free- Will- Offerings- Only doctrine of the old and new covenants mean you are only to give as you want to. Your free will gifts lead to blessings, but the tithe to the curse of OT law, (Gal. 3:10).

CURSES OF OT LAW

"For as many as are of the works of the law are under the curse; for it is written, "Cursed is everyone who does not continue in all things written in the book of the law, to do them" (Gal. 3:10). There are people who will read this in the bible and still not believe in the curse of OT law. When Father God gave Israel the OT law that placed them under the curse. OT law was a curse for man because of its righteous requirements. God could not lower His standards when giving His law. It was man's fallen nature that subjected man to the curse.

The only way for a person to do OT law and not be cursed was for them to obey the whole law. But only a righteous person could obey the whole law. Since all have sinned and come short of the glory of God no humans are righteous. Therefore, no humans could keep the whole law. But because of His righteous nature Lord Jesus was the only one who kept the law.

For an example of the curse of OT law at work consider Israel in the days of Malachi, prophet of God. Israel had been given the OT law of the tithe but refused to honor it. They would not give Father His ten percent of the harvests. Upset by the actions of some in the priesthood, and knowing Father used His tithe food to feed them, the people refused.

But Israel was in covenant with Father God, not His priests. Their refusal to honor the law was a refusal to obey their sovereign and the covenant that had in it provisions for the use of curses. Israel's refusal to be obedient to the command of God brought of them what some say is the worst of all curses, the drought. Although there are curses that do much hurt, droughts have been known to end more life than any.

NT TITHE?

"I will break the pride of your power; I will make your heavens like iron and your earth like bronze. And your strength shall be spent in vain; your land shall not yield its produce, nor shall the trees of the land yield their fruit" (Lev. 26:19,20). There is nothing like a drought, a curse of OT law.

The scheme to trick the NT Church into being cursed for using the OT law of the tithe is the work of satan's unholy trinity. It was put into action by their first using the tithe law in satan's fake church after changing the tithe from food to money. They were trying to bring about the destruction of Christ's Church in order to stop the spreading of the power of His new covenant.

Their grand scheme is to stop the coming of God's kingdom of righteousness by tricking the saints of the NT Church to adopt OT laws. That would place them under OT law (Gal. 3:12), instead of being empowered by the Spirit of God, which is what the fake NT tithe is all about today. Satan is trying to force Father God into sending His own saints to hell for rejecting Him and Lord Jesus by embracing the old obsolete covenant of law, instead of the New Covenant Lord Jesus gave His life to establish for them. And the deceived are willingly becoming tithers, tricked by the promises of more and fooled into thinking the OT tithe was given to the NT Church.

If the tithe is NT doctrine Father contradicted Himself. Because Father said, **"Behold, the days are coming, says the Lord, when I will make a new covenant with the house of Israel and with the house of Judah-not according to the covenant that I made with their fathers in the day when I took them by the hand to lead them out of Egypt"** (**Heb. 8:8,9**).

80

CURSES OF OT LAW

Father said the new covenant is not according to the old covenant, therefore nor is the NT Church. Because the new covenant is the NT Church's doctrinal foundation, not the old covenant, by Father God's own admission tithing could not be a doctrine of the new covenant nor the NT Church. And that's the reason why throughout all the scriptures of the NT you will never read that any NT Church ever had anything to do with tithing. Re-read the NT and see for yourself.

Satan, false teachers, protithers, and many who don't know they are working with satan have deceived vast multitudes with the NT tithe lie. This deception works so well because the people who come to what they think is Christ's Church, come seeking spiritual help. And they are very trusting of those they think are there to help them. Thinking as most do, if there is a place where a person is safe and free from danger to follow the lead of those there to help, love and guide them, surely it must be the church. It must be the house of God.

But most people fail to realize truth number one. It's not a house of God simply because it has a cross and the word Church on the building. People must remember satan is the great imitator. **"Beloved, do not believe every spirit, but test the spirits, whether they are of God; because many false prophets have gone out into the world"** (1 John 4:1) The Word says, **"the whole world lies under the sway of the wicked one"** (1 John 5:19). **"And the dragon was enraged with the woman, and he went to make war with the rest of her offspring, who keep the commandments of God and have the testimony of Christ"** (Rev. 12:17). To trick them into a curse.

81

NT TITHE?

Before they knew it many people had become members of groups that are cursed for use of the OT tithe law or other OT laws. Some even find out later they have joined an organization that is a daughter of Babylon the great, the mother of harlots. People who have their own agenda, using the church as a front. People who have absolutely no interest in Lord Jesus or the kingdom of God, their only interest is money.

That's why it's of the utmost importance that every believer become a truly dedicated student of the Word. Don't misunderstand, there are many people well worth listening to. People who have been gifted and charged by God with the responsibility to feed His flock. But there are also many who take this position to themselves, pretending to be what they are not for their own reasons. We cannot know for sure who is who just by looking. But there is something we can know for sure. The Holy Spirit will lead us and guide us into all truth. So regardless of who we are listening to we must make the Word of God, by the Spirit of God, our first and last authority. **"Be diligent to present yourself approved to God, a worker who does not need to be ashamed, rightly dividing the word of truth" (2 Tim. 2:15).** Feeding yourself with the Word of God daily.

The curses the ancient Israelites faced were spelled out for them, they were part of their covenant. They knew what to expect if they ever resorted to defiance of their God or the covenant they had with Him. But for those in Churches today whom satan has deceived into putting themselves under the curse of the law with the tithe, it was not easy to recognize. Because this satanic trick is camouflaged as church tradition.

82

CURSES OF OT LAW

The deception that causes the curse, the use of OT law, is still being taught in many so-called NT Churches as the right thing to do. Contributing to this blindness are church leaders who constantly urge the people, ("you have to pay your tithe") to do this bad religious tradition inspired by the devil. Over and over, they tell what is supposed to be a NT Church to do the OT law of the tithe, (Heb. 7:5). Blinded by the need or greed of money, they cannot see through satan's deception. They don't realize one of Christ's main reasons for coming to earth was to free mankind from faithless OT laws like the tithe, no longer of any use. Which our Lord did with His New Covenant.

"But when the fullness of time had come, God sent forth His Son, born of a woman, born under the law, to redeem those who were under the law, that we might receive the adoption as sons" (Gal. 4:4,5). But using the OT tithe law puts you back under the curse (Gal. 3:10). Stops you from being a Christian (Gal. 3:11). And places you under OT law (Gal. 3:12).

Many who have embraced the OT tithe think they are saints of the NT Church. However, because they continue to do faithless OT law (Gal. 3:12) they have placed themselves outside of the NT. It is by faith not law that a person is declared righteous by Father God. Adam and Eve's lack of faith in the things Father God had taught them led to their disobedience. Which brought the first curses and the fall of man, (Gen. 3:17).

Just as there are people unaware of their not being a Christian, there are also those who do not recognize being under a curse. Some have been cursed for so long they think it's just the actions of nature, something that just happens.

83

NT TITHE?

But when looking at very strange things that happen, to be truly focused we must look through the lens of God's Word. Our Lord said, **"I have come that they may have life, and that they may have it more abundantly" (John 10:10).** And yet there are so many who have never seen abundant life. Why? Because continued obedience is rewarded with abundant life, but continued disobedience brings punishments and curses. Man's disobedient nature has caused him many curses.

If our world had continued to be obedient to our creator, we all would be living the abundant life. But because of continued disobedience our world has been cursed with new diseases, the resurgence of old diseases, continual warfare, yo-yo economics, sexual slavery, foreign and domestic terrorism, daily homicides, ethnic cleansings, killer new drugs, resurging drug epidemics, continual racial tensions, and very questionable leadership worldwide. Curses, the high price of low living.

By our disobedience of a loving God and Father we have brought these things on ourselves. By allowing the deaths of millions of His children we now live in a world where all kinds of deaths have become commonplace because we are reaping what we have sowed. To ignore the living God and do whatever we want to do for the sake of money is to invite curses worse than these on ourselves. Curses were not part of the NT; however, they were part of OT law and, **"the man who does them shall live by them" (Gal. 3:12).** The tithe is OT law (Deut. 14:22). Satan designs his heresies and tricks around the Word of God because, **" God is not a man that He should lie, nor a son of man, that He should repent" (Num. 23:19).**

84

CURSES OF OT LAW

The people of the OT were given the law of the tithe, but because of the corruption of the priesthood and their doubts if their God really was God, doubts developed because of the many times Israel fell prey to other nations, Israel refused to make sacrifices and to tithe in the days of the prophet Malachi. These foods, then denied, were the means by which Father fed Priests and Levites (Num. 18:21-30). The reason Malachi was asking people to bring all the tithes into the storehouse.

Malachi's plea for the tithe foods was not to the NT Church. At that time (around 400 B. C.) there was no NT Church, nor would there be for over 400 years. The reuse of that OT plea in the NT Church is a satanically inspired bad religious tradition designed to trick God's children out of new covenant Holy Spirit power, and be cursed by use of OT law, (Gal. 3:10).

From an early age I was led into this bad religious tradition in my family church. Encouraged by my mother and father, both tithers, I became a tither. I knew nothing about the tithe except there were many people who tithed and said it was the right thing to do. For over thirty years I tithed, following man's tradition instead of God's Word. For all those years I was buying myself the curse of OT law, (Gal. 3:10). I didn't understand and no one ever explained to me that OT law was without faith or that doing OT law meant I would be living under OT law. But how could they explain to me that they didn't know? The only thing explained to me was the tradition. The only thing of importance to them, paying the tithe money. Walking with eyes closed by the lies of satan. Are you paying ten percent of your income to keep yourself under the curse of OT law?

85

NINE
WHERE BLESSINGS COME FROM

• • • •

"BEWARE LEST ANYONE cheat you through philosophy and empty deceit, according to the tradition of men, according to the basic principles of the world, and not according to Christ."
(Col. 2:28)

While having an on-the-job bible study with the group I affectionately came to know as "The Little Flock" there came to study with us a woman who said she was in a certain cult. She said she had never studied with anyone other than the people in the cult, but since this study was where she worked, she decided to study with us to see if anything was different.

"Can you tell us anything about this cult?" I asked because I had never been around anyone in that cult, to my knowledge. Nor had any of the others in the study. We were all a bit curious, to say the least. What is cult life like? Once she began, she talked about the cult for a long time. And when someone asked how the cult was financed? She said "we are taught to always be generous in our giving. But only give to the cult." "Whatever you do," she said, "must be done for the cult."

Because she was revealing these things in a bible study, I felt she might be reaching out for biblical help. Perhaps she was looking for vindication in the Word of God. Or maybe she had enough of the cult and was looking to scripture to help her find her way out. From her conversation I got the impression if she could have, she would have said more. From what I heard I felt sorry for her. And I think the others did too.

87

NT TITHE?

I felt I should try to help this woman if I could. Some days later we were on our break at the same time. I went over and sat at the table where she was, and we began to talk. Before long, our conversation was back on her cult. After a while she mentioned the cult's tithe. "I don't know much about that cult," I said, "but it never occurred to me that they tithed." She said, "Oh yes, we have to tithe because that's where our blessings come from." "O yes, no tithe-no blessings. You have to pay your tithe." "Everyone has to pay their tithe."

"Listen" I said, "do you not know that tithing was only for the old covenant? The new covenant has no tithe system. Under the old covenant the law of God gave the people ninety percent of all harvests. But the ten percent Father God kept for Himself so He could feed the Priests and Levites who worked in His sanctuary. He could not depend on those who also worshiped other gods, to take care of those who worshiped Him."

"The phrase "paying tithe" is misleading. It gives the impression the people were giving Father God ten percent of what they owned. But the law said they had to give God what belonged to Him. Father God made this perfectly clear when He said, **"And all the tithe of the land, whether of the seed of the land or of the fruit of the tree, is the Lord's. It is holy to the Lord. If a man wants at all to redeem any of his tithes, he shall add one fifth to it"** (Lev. 27:30,31). "If a person wanted to keep the tithe, they had to pay its value plus an added one fifth per cent. The value of the tithe and the added one fifth percent would be collected by the Levitical priests. It was their job, commanded by Father God, (Heb. 7:5)."

WHERE BLESSINGS COME FROM

"But that was under the old covenant. Father made that covenant with the people He had chosen to be His special people. But at that time those people had not chosen Father to be their only God. Father could not depend on them to do what they were supposed to do. They made a covenant with Father God promising to do all He had said, (Ex. 20:7). His number one commandment was that they have no other gods but Him. But in less time than it took Moses to go up Mt. Sinai and bring back God's commandments written out so He could teach them to the people, they had made themselves another god. Because Father could not depend on them, He made it law that they keep only ninety percent of all harvests and deliver ten percent of all harvests to Him. The ten percent belonged to God under OT law, **"according to the law" (Heb. 7:5)**".

"One of the most important things for those who study the bible to understand is, not everything in the bible was written to everyone, although everything in the bible was written for everyone. The laws of the tithe in the bible were not written to the people of the NT Church. However, the teaching from OT law that Father God requires accountability, a major lesson from that old covenant, was written for everyone."

"The laws of the old covenant, "I continued," were for the people of the old covenant. Because the Word of God is not studied as it should be, people don't see how satan and his false teachers misuse OT law to lead NT people astray. NT people were given the OT as a study tool only (1 Cor. 10:11). There is no better way to learn about covenant life with God than to study the life of others in covenant with God, (Rom. 15:4)."

NT TITHE?

"And by studying covenant life with Father God we learn the truth about the blessings of God. It is important that we know the how and why of God's blessings, because this is something the enemy uses to set would be Christians on the wrong path. They teach, as you said, that a person is blessed for tithing. But the Word of God says the tithe is OT law, (Heb. 7:5) and **"As many as are of the works of the (OT) law are under the curse" (Gal. 3:10)."** Is being cursed a blessing? Don't let the lies of the enemy continue to steal from you the many God given blessings that come with the truth of God's Word", I said.

"To be able to recognize the dark sinister nature of using OT tithe law to collect funds in the NT Church one would first have to be able to recognize the love and Christ likeness of giving voluntarily. Considering the many things our Lord has done for us, and what it has costed Him, does the use of a law to make us support Him even sound right? It's hard to believe how many satan has tricked with his NT tithe lie."

"You said your blessings come because you tithe. Listen my friend, we are never blessed by God for doing wrong. However, because He is the God of love, and because of His great compassion and mercy, He has been known at times to overlook our mistakes when He sees in our heart that we are trying to do what's right. And sometimes He blesses anyway. As king David said, **"Blessed is he whose transgression is forgiven, whose sin is covered" (Ps. 32:1).** When studying the bible notice that no one is ever forced to give anything they own to God. God blesses those who give because they want to give. Not because someone else needs or wants them to give."

90

WHERE BLESSINGS COME FROM

"But you must understand that those times when we are being blessed by God because He sees we are trying to do right will not last, because we have been given the knowledge of the truth, the Word of God. Only by the study of God's Word do we gain knowledge of the truth. And by learning from it how to do right, we continue to be blessed by God. It is a satanic lie that anyone is blessed because they tithe. Look to God's Word for truth, (2 Cor. 9:7). The fact that we are in the New Covenant and the tithe was in the Old Covenant should have raised some suspicion. And the fact that NT scripture reveals no involvement of the NT Church with tithing speaks loud and clear to those who have ears to hear."

"What you and I think about tithing, what your pastor or your mate thinks about tithing, or what anyone else thinks about tithing cannot compete with what God says about tithing. And God says tithing is a work of OT law, (Deut. 14:22-29). You must first recognize the tithe as OT law before you can understand why its use in the NT Church is so wrong, (Heb. 8:13). In (Matt. 23:23) Lord Jesus describes the tithe as OT law. Repeatedly the book of Deuteronomy declares tithing to be OT law, (Deut. 12:5,6). The writer of Hebrews (7:5) says the tithe is OT law. A fact recognized in all books of the Torah."

"One of the reasons Lord Jesus gave His life as a sacrifice was to free all people from OT law, (Gal. 4:4,5). So that we could be adopted by Father God into His family. Only those not using faithless OT law can be adopted. While straining out as a gnat NT doctrine, many swallowed the dangerous camel of OT tithe law. Believing man's word instead of God's Word."

91

NT TITHE?

"Because of satan's lies about a tithe, protithers are asking people to do what Lord Jesus gave His life to save people from, OT law, (Gal. 4:4,5). **"Therefore the (OT) law was our tutor to bring us to Christ, that we might be justified by faith. But after faith has come, we are no longer under a tutor" (Gal. 3:24,25)."** No longer under the OT law of the tithe."

"It was in satan's church of Rome that the tithe was renewed as money. This was done to entice the true Church to join this heresy. Which has caused what we see today, churches that claim to be of Christ but are faithless and powerless. Some of these go so far as to say the mighty works done at the beginning of the church age were only done then to show the church was of God. But the Holy Bible shows the mighty works of God being done throughout history. Churches become faithless and powerless by following satan in their lust for money and are tricked out of New Covenant power."

"Satan's plan to trick people out of NT power by tricking them into going backward by use of OT law, the tithe, has had success. And because his tricks are designed around the Word of God, and because God's Word is true, if man keep falling for satan's tricks his success will continue. And he will be able to keep those foolish enough to believe him in the condition people were in before the coming of Christ. Because God's Word says, **"Yet the (OT) law is not of faith, but "the man who does them shall live by them" (Gal. 3:12)."** And what is living by OT law but a return to the old covenant. And what is living under the old covenant but a return to pre-Christ conditions? Leading people away from the power of the New Covenant."

92

WHERE BLESSINGS COME FROM

"Satan could not handle one Jesus Christ. Now that there are millions each year being given the same Spirit satan is trying to stop all people from becoming Christians. That's why he continues trying to establish OT law in NT Churches. He has tried to put every OT law he could into the NT Church, but none has worked as well for him as the OT tithe. It has worked so well because his false church, the Roman church, changed the tithe from food to money. Insuring participation of the greedy."

I thought she would eventually say something, but she just sat there and listened. And every now and then she would give me a very strange look. I was beginning to feel like I was talking to myself. But I continued. "Did you know that tithers and people who do other OT laws can't figure out why the power of God's Word will not work for them? For them it's as if there was no cross of Christ, no victory won. Nor can they be soldiers in the army of the Lord. And they can't figure out why."

"Satan and his false teachers used on them the same tactics used on Adam and Eve in the garden, lies and a play on man's greed. The devil not only designs his tricks and heresies around the Word of God, but he uses God's Words in his lies to make them sound more believable. In the garden man was tricked with the promise of more power, **"and you will be like God, knowing good and evil"** (Gen. 3:5). And in the churches of today man is being tricked with the OT promise of a blessing, **"there will not be room enough to receive it"** (Mal. 3:10)."
"The use of the Word of God to make his lies sound more believable is one of satan's tricks that is rendered useless against those dedicated to Holy Spirit led bible study."

93

NT TITHE?

"It is disheartening to those who know the truth to be in a worship service when some leader encourages all people to do the OT law of the tithe. Father God made it perfectly clear that the new covenant, and therefore the new covenant's church is, **"not according to the (OT) covenant that I made with their fathers in the day when I took them by the hand to lead them out of the land of Egypt" (Heb. 8:9).** "But many hold on to this satanically inspired bad religious tradition."

"Our Lord came into this world and gave His life to save people by establishing a New Covenant (see Heb. 9:16,17), the greatest blessing of all. His New Covenant, containing His NT laws, are the means of redemption for those doing OT law, (Gal. 4:4,5). He was beaten beyond recognition, hassled and forced to carry the instrument for his demise. For six hours, naked and nailed to a cross, suspended between heaven and earth till dead, He pay the sin debt of many who reject His Word and accept the lies of His enemy. Disregarding what the bible says, they accept the fake tithe for money's sake. They will pay for rejecting God, God's Son, and God's Word."

"And as it is with you my friend, this satanic deception is so strongly believed by some that they think they are being blessed for doing what Lord Jesus gave His life to save them from. And have allowed their minds to be locked up in a house of bad religious traditions where all the windows are painted over with more satanic lies. So comfortable are they there that they refuse even to try to clean the windows so they can see the light of truth." **"Not everyone who says to Me, Lord, Lord, shall enter the kingdom of heaven" (Matt. 7:21).**

WHERE BLESSINGS COME FROM

With that her eyes widened, and I thought she was about to speak. But she didn't, so I continued. "Our Lord's victory over the works of the enemy insured the blessings we receive. Blessings far better than anything from the old covenant. That old covenant of law doesn't compare with the new covenant of peace and love. The OT was the covenant of retribution and that is where tithing takes you today. With the NT not only have we been given a better covenant, (Heb. 8:6) but along with it Father has imputed to believers the righteousness of Christ. And the grace of Almighty God our Father is ours."

"As His divine power has given to us all things that pertain to life and godliness, through the knowledge of Him who called us by glory and virtue, by which have been given to us exceedingly great and precious promises, that through these you may be partakers of the divine nature, having escaped the corruption that is in the world through lust" (2 Pet. 1:2-4). "Adding to that eternal life, how could the OT compare?"

At this point the lady seemed completely lost. She looked at me as if I was speaking a foreign language. Then suddenly, she gave me that defiant look and said, "I know that tithing is where my blessings come from, and I'm going to keep on tithing so I can keep on being blessed." I don't know who did this to her or if she did this to herself, but this woman was completely brain washed. And although they won't come out and admit it, there are many just like her. People brain washed into believing they can buy blessings from God with tithe money. Nothing could be farther from the truth. God's blessings, like His love, are free, and not for sell at any price.

NT TITHE?

That poor woman, like so many others, had been completely brain washed. And just as Lord Jesus said, it was **"making the word of God of no effect through your tradition which you have handed down"** (Mark 7:13). "The success of the fake tithe comes in part because false teachers present the tithe as NT doctrine to those who don't know the truth. And partly because many of these false teachers themselves, not knowing the truth, believe the tithe to be a teaching of the NT.

Although they have never seen any scriptural evidence of a NT tithe, they believe this because it is what they were taught. They believe it even though there are no instructions anywhere in NT scripture for the NT Church to tithe. Nor is it recorded anywhere in NT scripture that a NT Church has ever tithed, taught tithing, or had anything to do with tithing.

When a person has been taught what is not true as truth all their life, when the time comes for them to teach what can they teach except the untruth they were taught. For them that untruth has become their truth. As it most likely was for those who taught them. And those who taught them their tradition.

"All instructions for tithing are recorded in the books of the OT and nowhere else. The reason why they are recorded only in the books of the OT is because the tithe was only for the people of the OT. If tithing had been included in the NT, the instructions for a NT tithe would have been included in the scriptures of the NT. The fake NT tithe did not originate in the Christian Church. This diabolical heresy was started in satan's church. The church that stole the identity of Christ's Church and introduced a counterfeit Christianity, (see Jude 1:3)."

96

WHERE BLESSINGS COME FROM

"Did you know my friend, I asked, that the apostle Paul is credited with having written two thirds of the NT? Before becoming a Christian Paul was a Pharisee. Pharisees always tithed (Matt. 23:23), being dedicated to OT law. And yet after becoming a Christian Paul never even mentions a tithe. Not even when he oversaw the collecting of funds to assist the churches in Jerusalem who were in a famine. Do you think Lord Jesus forgot to mention a NT tithe to Paul in the years He was teaching him by revelations in the Arabian desert?" (Gal. 1:11,12).

"I tell you, there are many tithers who know the OT tithe is out of place in the NT Church. But because there are so many just like them, wrong but not willing to admit it, they find comfort in pretending not to know the truth. They simply are not strong enough to stand up against this long-held religious tradition. They are not strong enough because being imprisoned by satanic lies keeps them weak. That's the design and purpose of satan's lies. The more you accept the lies of the devil over the truth of God's Word the weaker you get."

"If you allow satan, his false teachers, or religious traditionalists to trick you into practicing any OT law (Gal. 3:12), you have been deceived and disqualified as a Christian. The New Covenant and its better promises (Heb. 8:6) will no longer apply to you. Faithless OT law is not for NT saints. NT saints are people of faith." **"Therefore, having been justified by faith, we have peace with God through our Lord Jesus Christ, through whom also we have access by faith into this grace in which we stand" (Rom. 5:1,2). "The (OT) law is not of faith, but "the man who does them shall live by them" (Gal. 3:12).**

NT TITHE?

The tithe is OT law. **"And indeed, those who are the sons of Levi, who receive the priesthood, have a commandment to receive tithes from the people according to the law"** (Heb. 7:5). "The OT priesthood collected tithes according to OT law. By doing the OT tithe, instead of free will giving, lifelong tithers have accepted satan's counterfeit Christianity. Sad is the fact that so many have accepted counterfeit Christianity without realizing its a counterfeit. They can't see that they have rejected the covenant Lord Jesus gave His life to establish for them by accepting doctrine from another covenant. Instead of using the doctrine of the NT, satan tricked them into using the doctrine of the OT, no longer a valid covenant, rejected by Father God over two thousand years ago, (Heb. 8:13)."

"Patted on the back and called good Christians, some people have tithed for many years, as I once did, not knowing they were doing OT law or what that meant for a follower of Christ. We were tricked into following along in the satanically inspired bad religious traditions of man instead of the Word of God. We were tricked, being taught by those who put the religious traditions of man ahead of God's Word. And money over truth."

"Because of that, some people walked away from the church and the Lord. They came to believe it was all a hoax. They came to this conclusion because of a time when they urgently needed God. They reached out to God, depending on their covenant affiliation to come through for them. But their affiliation was not with the true covenant of Christ. Because they had accepted satan's counterfeit they had no connection to the power of Christ's resurrection, NT Holy Spirit power."

WHERE BLESSINGS COME FROM

The lady in that cult and I had one more talk after that. She must have said something about our talks to someone in her cult. And apparently, they told her not to talk to me anymore. Although we worked in the same building, I didn't see her as often as before. Whenever I did see her, she would just wave hello and walk away. She never came back to another bible study, and she never talked to anyone in it again.

The last time we talked I told her how the Lord had rescued me from counterfeit Christianity and bad religious traditions. I told her how the Holy Spirit has impressed on me the same advice the apostle Paul had given his spiritual son Timothy. The old King James says it best. **"Study to shew thyself approved unto God, a worker that needeth not to be ashamed, rightly dividing the word of truth" (2 Tim. 2:15).** The knowledge of God's Word is the key, (2 Pet. 1:2-4). It will open the door that will free you from the confusion of satan's lies and the bad religious traditions of man. The Word of God is the light that illuminates the darkness of life lived in a sin filled world.

Our on-the-job bible study group stayed together for three years, and we studied from Genesis through Revelation. We made it a double study. As we went through the Word in general, we also made a special study of the tithe.

And we learned the importance of those in covenant with the Lord God living by the doctrine of that covenant only. Let me tell you how and why our blessings so lovingly come from Father God. **"And God is able to make all grace abound toward you, that you, always having all sufficiency in all things, may have an abundance for every good work" (2 Cor. 9:8).**

99

TEN
TITHING SELF TO DEATH

• • • •

**"YOU HAVE BEEN ESTRANGED from Christ, you who attempt
to be justified by law; you have fallen from grace" (Gal. 5:4,5).**

What do you think satan did after the resurrection of Christ? Do
you think he just threw up his hands and said that's it, he won? No,
not the devil. He is more determined than ever to destroy everything
that is anything to God. Having been judged and sentenced by Father
God already, satan knows it's just a matter of time before the flames of
hell become his eternal abode, (Rev.20:10). So, he seeks revenge now,
anyway he can.

He has tried many times to destroy Mother Israel, (Rev. 12:13-16).
But now he's trying to destroy everyone who **"keep the
commandments of God and have the testimony of Jesus Christ"
(Rev. 12:17).** He seeks to destroy Jews and Gentiles alike. As weapons
he has chosen to manipulate the laws and words of God. Satan has
no power over things that belong to God. But by his manipulation of
God's Word and laws he tries to trick God's children into destroying
themselves by their disobedience of God and belief in satanic lies, like
a NT tithe.

Satan uses lies, such as a person being blessed if they tithe, to
manipulate God's Word and laws because he has no other weapons.
Lord Jesus stripped him of his former weapons in His victory over satan
on a hill called Calvary. **"Having disarmed principalities and powers,
He made a spectacle of them, triumphing over them in it" (Col.
2:15).** Now satan designs his schemes, tricks, and heresies around the
Word of God.

101

NT TITHE?

Satan has success in tricking people by misusing the Word because he knows scriptures better than many Christians. He has misused the Word of God over and over down through the ages to confuse the masses. Which is why the study of the bible is so very important. Those who say they are a Christian but never study God's Word as He commanded (2 Tim. 2:15) walk around with a target on their back. And as brother John said, **"they are a liar, and the truth is not in them"** (1 John 2:4).

The devil is so familiar with the Word of God that he recited some of it to Christ in His temptations in the wilderness, (Matt. 4:1). Satan has a long history of manipulating the Word of God. His fake NT Church, the Roman Church, which he started with his unholy trinity was built on satanic lies and the manipulation of God's Word. Satan knows the Word of God has more power than anything he has ever said.

Lord Jesus said to the apostle Peter, **"You are Peter, and on this rock I will build My Church and the gates of Hades shall not prevail against it. And I will give you the keys of the kingdom of heaven, and whatever you bind on earth will be bound in heaven, and whatever you loose on earth will be loosed in heaven"** (Matt. 16:18,19). In their lying manipulations, satan, and his false priests, in his so-called NT Church of Rome claimed this declaration of Christ made the apostle Peter the head of the NT Church when Lord Jesus returned to heaven. The truth is, **"He (God) put all things under His (Christ) feet, and gave Him to be head over all things to the church, which is His body, the fullness of Him who fills all in all"** (Eph. 1:22,23). Christ is His Church's only head, forever.

TITHING SELF TO DEATH

The Roman church claimed this false authority after the death of the apostle Peter. They declared this authority from Christ was passed on to their church because Peter was its first Bishop. With this manipulation of the words of Christ, along with a multitude of other lies, dastardly deeds, financial corruptions, shameless involvements of the flesh, and many things more, the Roman church became the leading church of Christendom, The Mother Church. Lord Jesus said many would come in His name, and the devil was one of them.

As the mother of all churches, the Roman church, the undercover enemy of Christ's Church, assumed great authority due to the negligence of Christ's followers. With this authority they brought back the OT tithe system, dismantled by Father God when He removed all differences between Jews and Gentiles in the creation of His Church. But this tithe was different, not the food tithe of God. Money was substituted for food. It was done to entice money lovers to reject the titheless covenant of Christ, to tithe themselves to death, (Heb. 10:28,20).

Protithers set their congregations up for the Adam and Eve type fall we see happening today. It is sad to see the run down and abandoned condition of so many church buildings. But in those buildings congregations trampled the Son of God underfoot by ignoring His covenant and its doctrines. It seems they forgot He gave His life to secure these for them. The blinding love of money has made many worthy of punishment worse than death, (Heb. 10:28,29). For those deceived lovers of tithe money, intentionally leading souls astray to get it, what else could it be for them but the tithing of self to death?

NT TITHE?

In some so-called NT Churches, this bad religious tradition inspired by satanic greed has replaced the voluntary offerings doctrine Father God established in both the old covenant (Lev. 1:3) and the new covenant (2 Cor. 9:6). These leaders, with a false doctrine, a NT tithe, not only tell people they must give, but also how much they must give. The counterfeit of Christianity. **"And in vain they worship Me, teaching as doctrine the commandments of men" (Mark 7:7).**

Unless true children of God standup and speak out against the use of false doctrine in their church, man-made doctrine designed for the saving of dollars instead of lost souls and lead their people back to the God given doctrine of the NT Church, it will be lost. And they will be to blame. **"If the blind lead the blind, both will fall into a ditch" (Matt. 15:13).**

Any instructions you receive that are the opposite of what the Word of God says comes from the enemy, satan. The use of a tithe, an OT law (Heb. 7:5), in the NT Church is rebellion. The NT Church is not here to do what Father said for the people of the OT to do. The NT Church is here to do what Father said for the NT Church to do, (2 Cor. 3:5,6). NT use of OT tithe law is a trick to get the NT Church to reject NT law by use of OT law. Which is a rejection of Father God who established law and the rejection of Lord Jesus who fulfilled the law.

By promising people more if they become tithers, they are being turned away from the Free- Will- Offering- Only doctrine God gave to the old and new covenants. And in so doing turn Father God against those who have rejected His doctrine in the NT Church, (John 7:16). Satan trying to play both sides.

TITHING SELF TO DEATH

Satan's goal is to see God's children in hell with him. His scheme is to have God put them there Himself because of their disobedience of God, Christ, and the new covenant. That's what satan's counterfeit of Christianity is all about. It's designed to get people to reject what God is saying and believe the lies of satan. God has said in (Heb. 7:5) that the tithe is OT law. God has said in (Gal. 3:10) that anyone who does OT law is under the curse of the law. In (Gal. 3:11) God said if you do OT law you are disqualified from being a Christian. And in (Gal. 3:12) God says it's all because OT law has nothing to do with faith. But satanic lies say how much more you will have if you do this OT law. And many who call themselves Christians have been tithing all their life, believing satan's lies.

If you take a good look around some towns, you will see places where many congregations have been destroyed. How many of them do you think did not have being a tithing church in common? **"Do not be deceived God is not mocked; for whatever a man sows, that he will also reap" (Gal. 6:7).** If you reject God, He will reject you. **"He (Lord Jesus) said to them, "All too well you reject the commandment of God, that you may keep your traditions" (Mark 7:9).**

While attending churches over the years, I have seen many tithers who said they were Christians, but the power of God's Word didn't work for them. They did not realize they were, **"making the word of God of no effect through your traditions which you have handed down" (Mark 7:13).** They didn't know that tithing, living by OT law (Gal. 3:12), made them unjustified before God (Gal. 3:11), and disqualified as a Christian.

NT TITHE?

They didn't understand that a person is not a Christian simply because they want to be one, or just because they say they are one. They, like many others, only thought they were Christians. The power of God's Word works in the people of God. The power of the Holy Spirit is in everyone who is of God. **"But you shall receive power when the Holy Spirit has come upon you" (Acts 1:8).** But the satanically inspired bad religious traditions of man, like the NT tithe lie, were conceived by the devil to make the users powerless.

Protithe leaders either don't know or don't care that NT tithing is only a tradition with no scriptural support. NT doctrine says, **"He who sows sparingly will also reap sparingly, and he who sows bountifully will also reap bountifully" (2 Cor. 9:6).** Also, **"For with the same measure that you use, it will be measured back to you" (Luke 6:38).** In other words, what you give is always up to you. Not a tithe law from an old obsolete covenant that once belonged to people of a different faith, Judaism. That old covenant was rejected by Father God over two thousand years ago, (Heb. 8:13). There are well established reasons why one is called the Old Covenant and one is called the New Covenant, the everlasting covenant of Christ.

When the apostle Paul was talking to the church at Corinth about contributing to the relief effort for the churches of Jerusalem in a famine, he clearly noted the proper doctrine for NT offerings. Paul said, **"I speak not by commandment, but I am testing the sincerity of your love by the diligence of others" (2 Cor. 8:8).** Paul was reminding them that all NT offerings should be voluntary. Never forced, **"of necessity" (2 Cor. 9:7).**

TITHING SELF TO DEATH

Our Lord gave His life to establish a better covenant for us, (Heb. 9:16). With the new covenant our sins have been forgiven and we have been adopted into the family of the living God. But protithing false teachers are asking us to ignore our Lord's sacrifice, and for the love of money go backwards pass the cross to life under OT law, (Gal. 3:12). Those who do so and reward the money mad who teach people to ignore Father's Free-Will-Offerings-Only doctrine (Ex. 25:2) are buying themselves a very warm space for eternity.

There are so many protithers because there are so many people who love money more than they love God. Some people will do anything for money, their true god. False teachers have caused many to miss out on the abundant life that would have been theirs if they had followed the instructions of the NT instead of the bad religious traditions of man. **"And many will follow their destructive ways, because of whom the way of truth will be blasphemed" (2 Pet. 2:2).**

Lord Jesus said, **"My doctrine is not mine, but His who sent Me" (John 7:16).** Not only the doctrine for financial support in the NT Church, but all doctrine for both the old and new covenants came from Father God, Sovereign of covenants. To reject Father God's doctrine of voluntary offerings only, in favor of the temporary law of the tithe that was for Israel only, (Gal. 3:24,25) is like spitting on the face of Christ when He was hanging on the cross. **"Anyone who has rejected Moses' law dies without mercy on the testimony of two or three witnesses. Of how much worse punishment, do you suppose, will he be thought worthy who has trampled the Son of God**

107

NT TITHE?

underfoot, counted the blood of the covenant by which he was
sanctified a common thing, and insulted the Spirit of grace?" (Heb.
10:28,29).

Satan is deceiving tithers into throwing their eternal life away for
crumbs. Blinded by greed they do not see that the blessings God gives
extends far beyond mere money. **"For you know of the grace of our
Lord Jesus Christ, that though He was rich, yet for your sake He
became poor, that you through His poverty might become rich"** (2
Cor. 8:9). Those who understand this and do the will of our heavenly
Father are those who truly love Him and are blessed with, **"all things
that pertain to life and godliness, through the knowledge of Him
who called us by glory and virtue"** (2 Pet. 1:3).

There are those who don't believe a person can tithe themselves
to death. They think this because they don't understand what the use
of OT laws (Gal. 4:4,5) in the NT Church represents. Nor do they
understand the importance of the New Covenant. To them the use
of OT doctrine to replace NT doctrine is no big deal. But as sure as
water is wet this is a gigantic matter. A matter every member of the NT
Church should pay serious attention to. A sink or swim type matter.

With the use of the OT tithe law in the NT Church satan has
involved would be saints in his assault on the authority of Almighty
God. And in the belittling of the sacrifice of Lord Jesus. It is the
belittling of the sacrifice of God the Son's life. The sacrifice that entitled
Him and only Him to be the Mediator of His New Covenant. And the
only one entitled to implement any laws (Matt. 5:17,18) into His New
Covenant.

TITHING SELF TO DEATH

Father God made it clear, saying of the new covenant that it is, **"not according to the covenant I made with their fathers"** (Heb. 8:9). The old covenant, which had the tithing system, was Israel's national covenant, for Israel only. The new covenant is the covenant for the whole world. The covenant Father promised long ago, as far back as the days of Jeremiah His Prophet, **"Behold, the days are coming, says the Lord, when I will make a new covenant with the house of Israel and with the house of Judah"** (Jer. 31:31).

To bring this new covenant into the world meant the death of God's only begotten Son. Those who disregard the sacrifice of Christ, and for the money of a fake tithe prefer the doctrine of the obsolete old covenant over the doctrine of the everlasting new covenant, born of Christ's blood, are walking on His blood. And have considered the blood of Christ to be of less worth than the blood of the bulls and goats used in the OT.

While speaking with Moses Father said, **"I will raise up for them a Prophet like you from among their brethren, and I will put My words in His mouth, and He will speak to them all that I command Him. And it shall be that whoever will not hear My words which He speaks in My name, I will require it of him"** (Deut. 18:18,19).

NT tithers are not hearing God's words that Christ spoke in God's name. They hear the satanically inspired bad religious tradition of man. Those who because of tradition and money teach a tithe. A doctrine that had nothing to do with offerings. They are signing their own death certificate to satan's applause. Stiff necks who are tithing self to death.

ELEVEN
MAKE ALL GRACE ABOUND

••••

"AND GOD IS ABLE TO make all grace abound toward you, that you, always having all sufficiency in all things, may have an abundance for every good work" (2 Cor. 9:8).

At the age of ten when I joined the church, I was just following the crowd, being led by the actions of others whom I thought knew what they were doing. Years later, blessed with Holy Spirit led bible study, praise God, I began to hunger for more knowledge of the truth. The more I learned the more I wanted to learn. Before that I hadn't learned enough to realize that what some people said, and what the bible taught on the same subject was not always the same. But nothing prepared me for the shock when I learned about false doctrine used in the church for many years.

It really hurt me to realize that there were church leaders who did not care enough or did not know enough to defend the integrity of our God, His Church, and Christianity by addressing and correcting this long ago. Ministries that have allowed satan's counterfeit of Christianity not only to be used but also to strive among them for the sake of money should have all their members on their knees praying for God's forgiveness. But because their religious traditions have replaced the truth of God's Word, they can't see what's wrong. They have been taught the despicable lie that to do the OT tithe law is good, but the Word of God says those who do OT law, **"are under the curse" (Gal. 3:10).** Only one of satan's many lies.

111

NT TITHE?

The bible teaches that by the sacrifice of our Lord's life the NT Church has been given a better covenant. Never should you be persuaded to use the tithe doctrine from the old covenant that belonged to Judaism. The covenant declared obsolete by Father God over two thousand years ago. **"In that He says, "A new covenant", He has made the first obsolete" (Heb. 8:13).** When the love of God, by the sacrifice of His Son, gave the world a better covenant (Heb. 8:6), satan with his evil lies, playing on man's greed by promising him more, tricked many to adopt the old covenant. Can it be God's church that ignores God's instructions? Can it be God's church where money is more important than the Word of God?

How could so many people who say they are Christians remain obedient to traditions that teach them to do the opposite of what the Word of God says? It seems that surely, sooner or later, some bible believing person would think to ask the question, why? Why is the OT tithe law so vigorously taught in the NT Church? While Father's doctrine of voluntary financial support, recorded in both the old and new covenants, (Ex. 25:2), (2 Cor. 9:6) is so completely ignored?

The bible answers: **"For the love of money is a root of all kinds of evil, for which some have strayed from the faith in their greediness and pierced themselves through with sorrows" (1 Tim. 6:10).** And we were warned. **"But know this, that in the last days perilous times will come: For men will be lovers of themselves, lovers of money" (2 Tim. 3:1-3). "But there were false prophets among the people, even as there will be false teachers among you" (2 Pet. 2:1).**

112

MAKE ALL GRACE ABOUND

So how do those who have been led in the wrong direction get on the right track? How do you get to the place where the Lord wants you to be? Because everyone's relationship with the Lord is personal, and therefore different, no one can tell you exactly what you need to do. But I can tell you what I did. I went to my Lord in prayer, and I apologized for allowing people to steer me in the wrong direction. I admitted I should have been paying more attention to the Word of God than to the words of man. I confessed the sinfulness of my actions and prayed for God forgiveness. I prayed He would give me the wisdom and the strength to make the Word of God the first and final authority for everything in my life, always.

And I also prayed for those I had been listening to, those who said they knew the truth. I prayed they be forgiven also because they, like me and so many others, had been deceived by satan. The one **"who deceives the whole world" (Rev. 12:9).** They thought they knew the truth but were teaching the same bad religious traditions their misguided teachers taught them. Bad religious traditions are perpetually dangerous.

To have our offerings blessed by Father God, we must offer them according to His instructions. Father established and instructed us on how He accepts offerings with the very first offerings He accepted, saying: **"From everyone who gives it willingly with his heart you shall take My offering" (Ex. 25:2).** And the second offering, **"Whoever is of a willing heart, let him bring it as an offering to the Lord" (Ex. 35:5).** It is only what we give from our hearts that our God blesses from His heart. NT like OT offerings must be FREE WILL Offerings to be blessed.

113

NT TITHE?

As you study the NT notice the scriptures that speak of financial support always leave the amount given to the one doing the giving. A certain amount or percentage is never asked. And you have never in NT scripture ever read of a NT tithe. Father only accepts offerings that come from the heart. Both OT and NT offerings were to be done by love, not by law. Just as Father gave His voluntary offerings doctrine to the people of the OT, He gave the same to those of the NT.

"Give and it will be given to you: good measure, pressed down, shaken together, and running over will be put into your bosom" (Luke 6:38). **"On the first day of the week let each one lay something aside, storing up as he may prosper"** (1 Cor. 16:2). **"So let each one give as he purposes in his heart, not grudgingly or of necessity; for God loves a cheerful giver"** (2 Cor. 9:7). Father blesses offerings given from the heart.

We the heirs of God and co-heirs of Christ are not the ancient Israelites who were given the tithe that they **"learn to fear the Lord your God always"** (Deut. 14:23) Nor are we here to be taught how to be like them. We are here being taught how to be like Christ Jesus our Lord. Because **"the kingdom and dominion, and the greatness of the kingdoms under the whole heaven, shall be given to the people, the saints of the Most High"** (Dan. 7:27). We are being prepared to reign.

Because God is love we are children of love. We must learn to live by the motivations of love. No matter how much we give it will never match what we have received by love. Yet our voluntary offerings of love can produce results that mesmerize because of God's abounding grace.

114

MAKE ALL GRACE ABOUND

What I am going to tell you now comes from the heart of one who has learned to love truth. I tell you this with the Lord my God, the one who make these things happen as my witness. And in the name of the Lord Jesus, my Savior, I declare that this is all true. Not long after I stopped tithing and started giving according to NT doctrine wonderful things started happening in my life. Although I knew NT scripture says, **"God is able to make all grace abound toward you"** (2 Cor. 9:8), when this began it caught me by surprise.

Looking at my bank statement I did not believe what I saw. I almost called the bank to ask if this was a mistake. For the very first time I had money in my account at the end of the month. Usually, the money ran out long before the month did. Because of the suddenness of this I was momentarily baffled. But when similar things began to happen, I sensed the Holy Spirit speaking scripture, saying, **"And God is able to make all grace abound toward you, that you, always having a sufficiency in all things, may have an abundance for every good work"** (2 Cor. 9:8). I was witnessing the Word of God at work in my life.

The Holy Spirit showed me the NT tithe lie was **"conduct received by tradition from your fathers"** (1 Pet. 1:18). I have learned to give like King David, who said **"In the uprightness of my heart I have willingly offered all these things"** (1 Chr. 29:17). I now give from my heart, from love, not from OT law. As brother Paul said, **"For I through the law died to the law that I might live to God"** (Gal. 2:19). I no longer give according to an ancient law from an obsolete covenant that once belonged to a different faith (Judaism).

NT TITHE?

Having just moved and needing furniture I went looking for a rocking chair. I saw a used furniture store, so I went in to look around. There sat the most beautiful rocking chair I had ever seen. It not only rocked but it also swiveled. It was brand new. The price tag said three dollars. None of the other chairs looked half as good but costed much more. The salesman said it was the last one of its kind, so he priced it to go. Things like that happen to me all the time now. They never did when I was tithing. I know it's the Lord's favor, His making all grace abound toward me. God's love is the most amazing thing.

Being obedient to the new covenant of faith instead of the old covenant of law changed my life in ways my life would never have changed had I continued in the apostate traditions of counterfeit Christianity. I am not sure there are words that can adequately express what a person feels when they see the Almighty God working in their life. When they see God doing exactly what He said He would do if they only believed what He says. Can you imagine what that does for a person's faith?

"Therefore, I say to you, whatever things you ask for when you pray, believe that you receive them, and you will have them" (Mark 11:24). This is why satan tries to keep all people away from the new covenant. He doesn't want us to experience its amazing power. And he's doing that today with lies, the love of money, and false teachers. The Lord sent His disciples into the world. Satan sent his disciples into the church. The Lord died to give God's children a better covenant. Satan is trying to deceive us into accepting a substitute for the new covenant, which is a substitute for eternal life.

116

MAKE ALL GRACE ABOUND

The Lord directed me to a great rocking chair deal. But I had another problem. The house I moved into had no appliances. For weeks I had been taking my dirty clothes to a public washer. Then one day I got a call from one of my sisters. She wanted to know if I would come over and move her washing machine for her. She explained she was getting a new one and she needed to get the old one out of the way before the new one arrived the next day. She said she was getting a new machine because the old machine was leaking oil. The company she bought it from had sent out a repairman who after looking it over said it was at the end of its road.

After I moved the old washer to make room for the new one my sister said, "you can have it if you want it. It still works, it just leaks oil. Just take it home and use it until you get another one or it stops working."" Thanks, I said", and I took it home and started using it. That was four years ago and I'm still using it. And to this very day I have never seen one drop of oil come from under it. Often my sister asks how does it keep going?

Let me tell you something else God did for me after I started being obedient to my covenant and giving God's way. One day a family member whom I had not seen in a long time came to visit me. At the time I was under my car working on it. "Why don't you let the repair shop fix it" he said. "I like working on my car." "Besides", I said "they will charge four times what the repair is worth." "I can fix it", "I fix it all the time" I said, still under the car. "The fixing is the easy part; the hard part is finding out what's wrong." I did not come all this way from home to talk to two feet sticking out from under a car" he said.

NT TITHE?

"Look" he said "I'm going to call my auto club and have them send out a truck to take your car to the repair shop. Don't worry, I will pay for the repair. Will you please let me do this to help you. "OK, I said, if you insist, but remember I told you they will charge too much." "Listen, I got this" he said.

The truck came and we took my car to the repair shop. He told them to fix what was wrong with it. Although in somewhat of a mild shock I was beginning to recognize the Lord's hand. Once again, He was making all grace abound toward me. We walked around the showroom floor looking at new cars for a few minutes and then we left. On the way back to my house to wait for the repair shop to call he said, "what year is your car?" "It's a 01" I said. "That's an old car" he said. "Listen, in one week when I get back home, I will be picking up my new car." "I want you to have this car. It's all yours, all you need to do is come to the house and get it." "Wow, thank you" I said. "I can never thank you enough for all you have done for me today." He said "you are more than welcome, I'm glad I was here to help you. I've been told of the many people you help. And we all need help sometime." I thanked him again in between my thanks to the One I knew was really making this happen.

In all the years I was tithing I was never blessed like this before. At one time my tithe was the support of ten impoverished children in different nations. I had been taught it was the right thing to do, but it was wrong. Christ Jesus gave His life to redeem His Church from faithless OT laws. Because those who do faithless OT laws shall live by them (Gal. 3:12). I was doing the right thing, but I was doing it the wrong way.

MAKE ALL GRACE ABOUND

And something else happened that taught me more than anything the importance of remaining true to our covenant and having faith in its Holy Spirit power. The people in my family have been troubled with joint problems for many years. My mother, my brother, a sister, and cousins all had to have operations to replace joints. One day my mother said to me "you might as well get ready; it runs in the family." And not long after that day my joint problem began.

A friend told me about pills that rebuilt the surface of the joint bones. The deterioration of the bone's surface was the cause of the joint problem. I thought if I took these pills long enough, they would completely rebuild the bone's surface and eventually the problem would just go away. It did not. I took those pills for fifteen years and they were working ok. Until one night as I was sitting at home watching TV when a pain hit me like nothing I had ever felt before. The pain left me physically shaking and nervously wondering if another was on the way. I didn't know it then, but later the Holy Spirit led me to see that this excruciating pain was given to wake me up to the power within. Being a Christian, within me was the Spirit of Almighty God, the Spirit of Lord Jesus the Christ, the Holy Spirit. And yet here I was accepting this condition like others accepted it, because of what people said.

As soon as I regained my composure I called out to my Lord. I said, "Lord, your word says by my being in you I am a new creation (2 Cor. 5:17), and anything I ask in your name you will do, and it will give glory to Father God" (John 14:13). "Lord, I ask in Your name that all the joints of my body be healed."

119

NT TITHE?

I said "Lord I ask this believing Your Word. I am a new creation in Christ. Therefore, I don't have to live with the old ailments of my earthly family. I now Lord, according to Your Word, lay my hands on these joints to represent all my joints, and in your name Lord Jesus I say to my joints that they be healed and made perfectly well, in Christ Jesus name." I got into bed and slept like a baby. Before I got out of bed, I knew I had been healed. Before my feet hit the floor. How? **"The Holy Spirit also witnesses to us" (Heb. 10:15).**

That was over seven years ago, and I have had no more problems with my joints. In fact, since then I have been healed of many other problems as well. Nothing is too hard for God; all you need is faith in Him. Instead of having faith in the satanically inspired bad religious traditions of man. But do not take my word for it, take God's Word. Ask Him to lead and guide you each time you study the bible. Every day, you can. The more God you put in you; the more of this world and satan you take out of you. You feed the flesh every day, and the flesh is an enemy (1 Pet. 2:11). We need to feed our Spirit (ourselves) everyday as well to keep us stronger than the flesh. Only then will we be able to lead the flesh instead of the flesh leading us.

Talk to God, He is our loving Father. Ask Him to show you if you are supposed to tithe. The truth of God's Word is within your reach, all you need to do is accept it. From it you will learn one of the greatest lessons in life. If you put God first in your life, **"God is able to make all grace abound toward you, that you, always having all sufficiency in all things, may have an abundance for every good work" (2 Cor. 9:8).**

120

TWELVE
THE HEART TEST

• • • •

"I KNOW ALSO, MY GOD, that You test the heart and have pleasure in uprightness" (1 Chr. 29:17).

When a person stops putting the OT tithe law from the obsolete covenant of the ancient Hebrews (Heb. 8:13) ahead of their own covenant with God through Christ and began to be financially responsible according to the doctrine of the NT its best if they initially keep it to themselves. Because it's hard to go against what you have been taught all your life. And it will be made more difficult by disapproving people trying to stop you. And they will try to stop you if they know what you are doing because they think they are right, even though they are wrong. They have not seen the light, but when they do, they too will thank God that they like you are out of the darkness.

As enlightened people continue to use NT doctrine instead of OT doctrine and see the results of doing things the new covenant way, out from under satanic deception, no one can stop them from telling it. Protithers have been deceived into rejecting NT doctrine by believing satan's lies of getting more with a tithe, blinded by greed. They don't know the NT tithe lie is a satanic deception started long ago to infest the NT Church with OT law (Gal. 3:10-12). They have not realized that this is the reason so many churches are failing today. People are creatures of habit and naturally hold on to long held traditions. Which is why satan and the powers of darkness create bad religious traditions like the fake NT tithe.

121

NT TITHE?

The true tithe was totally different from what people are taught today (Lev. 27:30-32). So-called NT Churches that tithe send out a message that you can use OT laws in the NT Church. But they don't use the OT law of circumcision in their church. Nor are the OT Kosher Food laws welcome there. And if OT laws are accepted in the NT Church today where are the animal sacrifices that were such a large part of OT law? And what about the OT Levirate marriage law? OF all OT laws it's only the OT tithe law that money loving protithers insist on using.

"For as many as are of the works of the law are under the curse; for it is written, "Cursed is everyone who does not continue in all things which are written in the book of the law, to do them. But that no one is justified by the law in the sight of God is evident, for "the just shall live by faith." Yet the law is not of faith, but "the man who does them shall live by them." (Gal. 3:10-12). Christ has redeemed from OT law those who no longer use them (Gal. 4:4,5).

Sharing in the financial expenses of the NT Church is both privilege and blessing. But these God given privileges and blessings only operate according to the doctrine of Father God. Lord Jesus revealed **"My doctrine is not Mine, but His who sent Me" (John 7:16).** Father's doctrine for accepting offerings in the NT is the same doctrine He had in the OT. **"For I am the Lord, I do not change" (Mal. 3:6).** In the OT He said: **"From everyone who gives it willingly with his heart you shall take My offering" (Ex. 25:2).** In the NT He said: **"So let each one give as he purposes in his heart" (2 Cor. 9:7).** We should always offer what our hearts say, not what other people say.

THE HEART TEST

In both previous verses we see the word "heart", what we share with others always reveals our heart. Among men we encounter the tests of wills, but with Father God there is the test of the heart. He only accepts what we voluntarily give from our hearts. The same way He gives to us (John 3:16). The same way Lord Jesus gave Himself for us (John 10:18).

Do not be confused, as so many have been, by listening to what false teachers and the misinformed have to say. Get your instructions from the Word of God. Be like the people of Berea who checked out with scripture whatever information came their way (Acts 17:10,11). The tithe was not an offering, it belonged to God, (Lev. 27:30-32). Ten percent of all agricultural harvests God reserved for Himself. Satan, through his fake NT Church of Rome, twisted the facts trying to make all people think they had to tithe, to get all to do OT law. Because the use of OT law disqualifies people from being justified by Father God (Gal. 3:11) and becoming a Christian. Having what satan fears most, NT Holy Spirit power. Having God within.

Many church doors have closed for good. Church buildings are now being used for other purposes and being torn down. When people see closed churches, they wonder why. Though there are many things that could end a congregation, there is one thing that will do it every time, false religion. It has been the knife to the heart of religious people for eons. False religions never last because they have untruths as their foundation. Some are groups that form for love of money. They only pretend to be of God. They come crashing down, never being able to pass God's test of their hearts.

123

NT TITHE?

For every ten church buildings you see that have closed their doors for good, if you ask former members if they were a tithing church nine or ten out of the ten will say yes. Meaning they were trying to use OT law in what was considered a NT Church. In other words, they were doing what Father God told the people of the OT to do, instead of doing what Father said for them to do. Listening to satan's lie that they could get more by doing what God told them to do some other way. Satan's same old lies. And people still believing them.

Some people after recognizing the sinfulness and lovelessness in themselves will try to do something about it. So, they join a church, attend regularly, and pay tithes, paying attention to the traditions of man more than the Word of God. They don't know they are doing exactly what the powers of darkness want them to do. What they have started by becoming a NT tither is a new problem, it's the problem of all who leap before they look. And many leap into a tithe before looking to see what the Word of God says about the matter.

Some people are hypnotized by satan's counterfeit Christianity. And coerced into doing what man says instead of what God says. **"And in vain they worship Me, teaching as doctrines the commandments of men"** (Mark 7:7). All of man's bad religious traditions come from satan, the father of the lie. Lord Jesus said, **"If you abide in My word, you are My disciples indeed. And you shall know the truth, and the truth shall make you free"** (John 8:31). And **"He who does not love Me does not keep My words; and the word which you heard is not Mine but the Father who set Me"** (John 14:24).

124

THE HEART TEST

Most of the closed tithing churches had one thing in common. They lacked a foundation of true love for God and their fellowman. Not having this, but protithers who teach a false doctrine, they could never pass Father God's test of the heart, (Chr. 29:17). Our God is the God of love. Love lives in hearts in line with God's heart. People who do not love are people who do not know God. And people who do not love are not interested in God's test of their heart.

But if you have accepted Lord Jesus as your Lord, if you have been baptized in His name (Gal. 3:27), His life is now your life and your life is now His life, you **"have put on Christ" (Gal. 3:27).** And **"as He (Christ) is, so are we in this world" (1 John 4:17).** Which means His covenant is our covenant. And we are expected to keep our covenant obligations by doing what our covenant says, not what someone else's covenant said. We must do what Father God, our covenant Sovereign, has given us to do. Learning to do what God has given you to do is the key to a very successful life.

Deceived protithers will continue to be protithers. They refuse to admit they are wrong; they refuse to honor voluntary offerings only. They don't seem to understand the more you voluntarily give the more you get. **"He who sows sparingly will also reap sparingly, and he who sows bountifully will also reap bountifully" (2 Cor. 9:6).** It's all about the heart and love, not law. Father doesn't need what we have, He gave it to us. He uses as a gauge our heart when giving us more. If when standing before Christ He asks why you rejected voluntary offerings, what will you say, knowing He's testing your heart?

125

THIRTEEN
FOR THE LOVE OF MONEY

. . . .

"THIS HE (JUDAS ISCARIOT) said, not that he cared for the poor, but because he was a thief, and had the money box; and he used to take what was put in it" (John 12:6).

Before my extensive study of Israel's tithing system with the study group called "The Little Flock", I was a construction worker. One block over from the warehouse where our construction team would meet was one of the most beautiful buildings I had ever seen. Although it was an older building it was still the most beautiful one around. A very large sign on it read CHURCH. It also had a very large cross.

Each time I passed by this church there was something about it that drew my attention, but I just couldn't make out what it was. At first, I thought it was only the beauty of the building that sparked my interest and the desire to see more of it that kept drawing me. But later I sensed there was something more, perhaps something for me to learn.

And so, one Sunday, my curiosity having peaked, I went to this church to worship with people I did not know and had never met. When I walked into the building they were already in service. I took a seat as close to them as I could. As soon as I sat down a woman sat down next to me. And with a smile from ear to ear she said, "Good morning, I am the pastor's wife, and I am so glad you have come to worship with us today." "What is your name" she asked. And after I told her she said, "mister I hope you are looking for a church to join, and if you are, you

127

NT TITHE?

have come to the right place. This is a family church and a great place to worship. Ask anybody and they will tell you the same thing, a great church indeed."

Moving even closer and slightly lowering her voice she asked, "do you work in this area? What kind of work do you do?" Before I could get a word in, she continued, "does the company you work for pay well? Are they hiring now? I'm asking you these things, she unashamedly said, because our church is looking for tithers. Oh yes, she said, as if an afterthought, are you married? Or perhaps looking for that special someone" she said with a smile. "We have some wonderful single women here who are looking for a good man to marry." "Yes sir", she said, "this is a great church, ask anybody." I could tell by the way she spoke all this was well rehearsed.

It was then revealed to me by the Holy Spirit why I had been drawn to this church. I was here to witness what was going on. After several more visits to churches very similar to this church it became clear to me. My Lord was preparing me to be a witness for something He was going to do. I learned He was preparing me to be of assistance in His writing of this book. While studying the tithe I was shocked to learn just how little tithers knew about tithing. And even more shocked later to learn that satan in his demonic schemes uses laws of the old covenant, like the tithe law, in his attempt to bring about the downfall of Christ's Church and the eternal death of all its members. My Lord was allowing me to witness this satanic deception in different churches. And see how satan uses the religious traditions of man as ropes that bind man to his lies.

FOR THE LOVE OF MONEY

As I sat there amazed by what the woman had said, and even more amazed by what had not been said about reasons to join this or any church, a man came over and sat down next to me. I noticed the pastor's wife, after talking to me, went to this man and whispered in his ear. He introduced himself and I told him who I was. He said the pastor's wife had asked him to come over and talk to me and tell me what a wonderful church this is. And he did. He went on and on about how wonderful the church was and how very happy it had made him since he joined. After what seemed like a very long time he stood up, shook my hand, and went back to his seat.

With the pastor's wife's one tract mind on money disturbing my spirit I started to get up and walk out the door, but I didn't. At first, I thought I was just being polite by not walking out the door. But later I realized it was the Holy Spirit directing me to stay because I had not seen all I was brought here to see. And there was more to see than I could ever have imagined.

There were two men seated on the podium. One was an older man, the other man was the pastor, a few years younger than the older fellow I guessed. The older gentleman got up, took the microphone in his hand, and began to give his testimony. He began by thanking God for all the many things He had done for him over the years of his life. The people were really into what the old man was saying. There were loud shouts of encouragements and amens from all over the church. The people were all clapping their hands in strong support to affirm all the old gentleman was voicing. Anyone could tell the old man was revealing what was in his heart.

NT TITHE?

This continued for a good five or six minutes when all of a sudden, the pastor jumped up, snatched the microphone out of the old man's hands and proceeded to scream and shout over and over "Aint He alright" "Aint He alright". Over and over, he kept screaming and shouting the same thing, "Aint He alright" "Aint He alright". In all my years of attending church, well over half a century, I had never witnessed anything like this before. It seemed like I was the only one shocked.

After about three or four minutes of this "Aint He alright" sermon, that had no scriptural reference or tittle, no biblically outstanding points, and no supporting characters, all at once, as if on cue all the people joined in with the same "Aint He alright" "Aint He alright". They began standing, running the aisles with flailing hands, having a screaming, shouting, hand clapping, ear piercing, house shaking "Aint He alright" good time. This went on for about five or six minutes and then ended as abruptly as it had started. They all calmed down and that was that. That was the pastor's sermon and the congregation's spiritual contribution all in one. I could not help but wonder where in the world did these people come from.

Then they passed the plates to take up the offerings. After which the tithers were asked to come forward, the OT words of Malachi once again ringing in their ears, "Will a man rob God?" Followed by the ever familiar, "Bring all the tithes into the storehouse." Then they so dutifully went to the place where they gave a tenth of their income each week. And after the money for the building fund, the money for the picnic, and then money to help the local candidates for election.

FOR THE LOVE OF MONEY

I sat there totally stunned, wondering if what I had just witnessed was real. Following a five minute, I guess you would say sermon, of three words "Aint He alright", the collecting of funds went on for twenty minutes. For the members of this well fleeced congregation the real message went unseen and unheard. In my extreme state of amazement and unbelief I stood up and walked out of fairyland. As I was walking out, I couldn't help but notice all the smiling faces. Which reminded me of the words of Jeremiah, **"The prophets prophesy falsely, and the priests rule by their own power; and My people love to have it so. But what will you do in the end?" (Jer. 5:31).**

A sermon was not all that important. The true focus was money. The pastor nor his wife even mentioned God or Christ by name. "Aint He alright" was as close as they came. Nothing was said about the sacrifice of Christ, getting saved or being born again. Salvation was never mentioned, nor the price paid for mankind's forgiveness of sins. No words were spoken about what children needed to learn about the living God. Nothing was said about the Word of God or its power in the life of Christians. And I guess they just didn't have time to pray.

It's hard to understand how a person who goes looking for the light of God can accept and then become so at home in satanic darkness. But this is what happens to those who have not studied the Word of God enough to know the difference between the satanically inspired traditions of man and the true doctrine of God. I found myself among people pretending to be a church of God for the love of money. These con artists had convinced this congregation that they were righteous servants.

NT TITHE?

"For such are false apostles, deceitful workers, transforming themselves into apostles of Christ. And no wonder! For satan himself transforms himself into an angle of light. Therefore, it is no great thing if his ministers also transform themselves into ministers of righteousness, whose end will be according to their works" (2 Cor. 11:13-15).

A little learning is truly a dangerous thing. Protithers do not know the truth about tithing. They have been taught that this bad religious tradition of man was put in the NT Church by God. And they refuse to accept anything different. Their eyes are closed to everything except a ten percent tithe. Which in the long run will cost them more than they ever could have imagined. "It is a fearful thing to fall into the hands of the living God" (Heb. 10:31). "Vengeance is Mine, I will repay, says the Lord" (Heb. 10:30).

Protithers ignore the fact that all instructions to tithe are recorded only in the OT. To them it makes no difference that the OT was declared obsolete as a covenant by Father God over two thousand years ago (Heb.8:13). And they ignore the fact that the OT was replaced by the NT. Being blinded by greed or need, they can't see that satan wants them to spread his NT tithe lie so that eventually God will have to destroy them for leading people astray by teaching false doctrine.

He lost his authority, so satan schemes to trick people to go against the authority of God. And having dealt with mankind for centuries satan knows he can do this through man's greed. So, he uses money around the world because there is nothing some people won't do for the love of money.

FOURTEEN
VOLUNTEERISM

• • • •

"THEN THE LORD SPOKE to Moses, saying: Speak to the children of Israel, that they bring Me an offering. From everyone who gives it willingly with his heart you shall take My offering" (Ex. 25:1,2). "So let each one give as he purposes in his heart, not grudgingly or of necessity; for God loves a cheerful giver" (2 Cor. 9:7).

Volunteerism is all about hearts that love. The New Covenant came to be because God loves people so much that He volunteered the love of His life, His only begotten Son, to establish it. The salvation of all God's children came because of this voluntary gift. When speaking about the sacrifice of His life for you and me Lord Jesus said, **"No one takes it from Me, but I lay it down of Myself"** (John 10:18). In total agreement with Father God Lord Jesus volunteered His life. Father also volunteered His Holy Spirit. **"But the Helper, the Holy Spirit, whom the Father will send in My name, He will teach you all things, and bring to your remembrance all things that I said to you"** (John 14:26). Volunteering to help is the essence of love.

Volunteerism is the foundation and the main doctrine of the New Covenant and the new covenant's church. Just as it was the foundation and main doctrine of the old covenant and the Temple. Volunteerism is as important in the NT Church as it was in the Tabernacle and the Temple. Although law is a tool Father God uses in the development of people, because He is love volunteerism is His natural way.

133

NT TITHE?

Because **"God is love"** (1 John 4:8) it is not in His nature to demand offerings for Himself. **"Love does not seek its own"** (1 Cor. 13:5). All contributions to His Church, financial and otherwise, should be given the only way He accepts them, voluntarily, (Ex. 35:5), (2 Cor. 8:8). Not according to OT law, the tithe, which had nothing to do with offerings. But was used as such by satan's unholy church of Rome to lead people astray.

"But now we have been delivered from the law, having died to what we were held by, so that we should serve in the newness of the Spirit and not in the oldness of the letter" (Rom. 7:6). Satan tries to get us to do anything other than what our Lord has said for us to do. The NT Church's obedience to the OT doctrine of the tithe as an offering is its disobedience of God's free-will- offering-only doctrine. The offering doctrine Father God established in both covenants.

Lord Jesus said, **"It is more blessed to give than to receive"** (Acts 20:29). More people would understand this if they knew the truth as King David did. And had the right attitude when giving for the work of the Lord. Because he knew the truth and had the right attitude King David gave Father much praise saying, **"O Lord our God, all this abundance that we have prepared to build You a house for Your Holy name is from Your hand and is all Your own. I also know, my God, that You test the heart and have pleasure in uprightness"** (1 Chr. 29:16,17).

A person reveals their true self by the way they give. When we give voluntarily by faith, we show the depth of our love. We affirm our dedication to our covenant and how much we appreciate what Father is doing in and through us. On the other

VOLUNTEERISM

hand, those who use the OT tithe law in the NT Church as an offering are showing the Lord that they have more respect for the bad religious traditions of man than they have for the Word of God and their own covenant. They show that they care more for a law from an obsolete covenant (Heb. 8:13) than they care for their own covenant with the One who gave His life for them. Or that they just don't know what they are doing. Which, unfortunately, is the case with so very many.

Some people have been deceived for so long by satan's trick, not being able to rightly divide what the Word meant when it said not to give **"of necessity" (2 Cor. 9:7)**. Some have been involved in this satanic heresy for so long that regardless of what the bible says they refuse to believe NT tithing could be wrong. And then there are those who know it's wrong.

They know we don't owe Father God ten percent because He has freely given us all things (Rom 8:32). All things that pertain to life and godliness (1 Pet. 1:3). Father gave Israel only ninety percent of all harvests because He could not trust them to feed His priesthood, widows, orphans, and the poor and needy. He could not trust them to do this because they also worshiped idol gods. So, Father had His priests collect His ten percent (Heb. 7:5), store it in His Temple and share it as He instructed. The tithe was not an offering, it was God's.

Volunteerism is the forever doctrine of Father God and those who are His. It is the way love operates. But satan, through his false teachers spread his NT tithe lie knowing sooner or later, as God judged Israel's idolatry, God will also judge today's churches that use the tithe as an offering.

NT TITHE?

Lord Jesus gave His life to redeem people from OT law by creating the New Covenant. This New Covenant that was promised by Father God (Jer. 31:31) is the covenant of Peace, Faith, Love and Grace. Its where we, members by adoption into God's family, have forgiveness of sins and an inheritance as sure as heaven itself. And God's Church, which has this new covenant as its foundation, has a covenant unparalleled. **"But now He has obtained a more excellent ministry, inasmuch as He is also Mediator of a better covenant, which was established on better promises" (Heb. 8:6).**

However, because of satanic deception today's protithers fight against God's doctrine of volunteerism. The doctrine Father established in both the old (Ex. 25:1,2) and new (Mark 12:41) covenants. For deception, satan, through his false church of Rome, reintroduced the OT tithe, which had nothing to do with offerings, as an offering doctrine. Because they have been deceived today's protithers have accepted this bad religious tradition, a product of the church of satan. Its purpose is to get as many people as possible to do OT law (Gal. 3:10-12). Which places all users (Gal. 3:12) outside of NT power.

I have learned that many Christians know very little about the church of satan. Some don't know satan has a church. And many have no idea of the impact it has had on the true Church of Christ. Some are members of satan's church and don't know it. They made themselves members of satan's church when they rejected God's doctrine, volunteerism, and accepted satan's doctrine, a fake NT tithe. For when they rejected the doctrine of God, they rejected the God of the doctrine.

VOLUNTEERISM

The people satan has tricked into using the OT tithe in the NT Church do not understand that satan is doing this so it can be used against them. Just as he did with Adam and Eve satan uses his lies and tricks to turn us against the instructions of Father God so that Father, because He is righteous, will have to judge us. This is how he got Adam and Eve put out of the garden of God. And this is how he got the Israelites put out of the promise land. Not by satan's power but by man's weakness. And man's unwillingness to stand with God.

The Israelites knew Father had said, **"You shall have no other gods before Me" (Ex. 20:3).** But because of satanic influence they envied the gods of the pagans around them. They became more interested in the nations Father warned them not to be like, than they were interested in becoming the nation Father had called them to be. Likewise, tithing churches know Father God has said the new covenant is **"not according to the covenant that I made with their fathers" (Heb. 8:9).** They also know that NT scripture does not endorse a tithe. But like the ancients they want to do what those around them are doing. **"For they loved the praise of men more than the praise of God" (John 12:43).** And just like the ancients they will pay a high price for ignoring the Word of God.

Most churches teach the bible and its history only. But what about the things that happened after the bible was written? What about the things that happened after that had such significance that they changed the way people thought before. There are things that happened after the bible was written that are as important as the things that happened before.

NT TITHE?

When we study history after the bible was written, we are given amazing insights all Christians need. Such historical study shows how Father God's doctrine of free-will-offerings only was changed for the OT tithe law in the Roman church of the fourth century A. D. The whole history of the Church is important because of the many things that shaped the Church into what it is today. Things done in the Church and out.

Other than the true Church of Christ the most outstanding contributor to Christianity, although its contributions are negative, is the church of Rome, satan's church with its counterfeit of Christianity. Make no mistake, there was then just as there is now, the church of satan. Because of the lack of teachings on the history of Christ's Church from its beginning to the present there is much vital information many saints are unaware of. Information all Christians need to know. But we can gather some knowledge from secular studies. In (2 Tim. 2:15) Paul said to study. He did not say the bible only. There are several secular fields that contribute well to biblical knowledge.

Secular history speaks of the infamous Roman church. The Emperor of Rome, Constantine, who was not a Christian, but a worshiper of the sun, because he was the emperor made himself the head of that church. Secular history tells how this false church used lies, sexual immoralities, murders, and the deplorable use of money to manipulate its way to the very top of church leadership. The Lord sent His disciples into the world, the devil sent his disciples into the church. Only God can truly tell one group from the other, the saints in the world from the devils in the church. **"Let both grow together"** (Matt. **13:30**).

VOLUNTEERISM

By satanic deception, pretending to be of God, with unholy use of money, their true god, with the emperor and all the heads of roman government in it, this fake church gained the highest position in organized religion, The Mother Church. As the mother church it had the authority to both make and change church doctrines. They made it illegal for common people to own or even read the bible. And then they changed the language of the church to Latin while moving the church away from the doctrines of God.

Because of their greed they not only wanted to make people give, but by bringing back the OT tithe laws they could tell people how much to give and when. The predecessors of today's protithers ruled and reigned from the church of satan while claiming that it and all that it did was of God. Just as Adam and Eve had been deceived into giving their allegiance and dominion authority to the evil one, now the church world had been deceived as well. This is where it all began, the heaven-bound Church's struggle with hell bound impostors. Because satan was not able to destroy the Church from the outside he changed his strategy to try from the inside by creating a church and a counterfeit Christianity of his own.

As the apostle Jude said, **"I found it necessary to write to you exhorting you to contend earnestly for the faith which was once for all delivered to the saints. For certain men have crept in unnoticed, who long ago were marked out for this condemnation, ungodly men, who turn the grace of our God into lewdness and deny the only Lord God and our Lord Jesus Christ"** (Jude 1:3,4).

139

NT TITHE?

Once the impostor church had ascended to the highest position of church leadership, mother of all churches with the highest authority, then church changes began to flow. Because they did not want to give Father God credit for being the creator of all things who hallowed the seventh day, they changed their Sabbath to the first day of the week. The sun worshipers Sunday. And after changing the fourth commandment they changed the second to allow themselves to worship things of their choosing. And to stop people from becoming Christians by tricking them to use OT law (Gal. 3:11), they rejected Father God's law of a tithe of food and substituted with a tithe of money. Which became the tradition many teach as doctrine.

The tithe law, a law that separated Jews from Gentiles had been blotted out (fulfilled) by Christ along with all OT laws. **"Having wiped out the handwriting of requirements that was against us, which was contrary to us. And He has taken it out of the way, having nailed it to the cross" (Col. 2:14).** And He has given us NT law, also known as the law of Christ. But that has not stopped satan from using his NT tithe lie to get mankind back under law where they will be weak and away from the power of the New Covenant. Even though Father's free-will doctrine is everywhere in NT scripture. Where a verse that connects the NT Church with tithing can't be found.

With his false Christianity satan stops people from being real Christians by tricking them to live by that which has nothing to do with faith, OT law (Gal. 3:12). He does this for several reasons, but his number one reason is to stop them from receiving the spiritual power they will get in the New Covenant.

VOLUNTEERISM

Father has already condemned satan to life in hell (Rev. 20:10), but he still fights, trying to change the conditions in the hope that it will change the outcome. He's trying to stop people from being NT saints so he can stop them from taking over all the kingdoms of the world. **"Then the kingdom and dominion, and the greatness of the kingdoms under the whole heaven shall be given to the people, the saints of the Most High. His kingdom is an everlasting kingdom, and all dominions shall serve and obey Him"** (Dan. 7:27).

Those who tithe in the NT Church are living by OT law (Gal. 3:12). That's why the power of the New Covenant will not work for them. Volunteerism is of God, and it works hand in hand with faith in God. If you have been deceived by protithing preachers and teachers don't be too hard on them, after all, they have been deceived also. **"So the great dragon was cast out, that serpent of old, called the Devil and Satan, who deceives the whole world"** (Rev. 12:9).

Remember, we have a loving and forgiving Father who says to those who have been led astray **"Return to Me and I will return to you"** (Mal. 3:7). The NT Church is a family of forgiven, God loving, volunteers. And just as everything else in the NT Church is done voluntarily, we are instructed throughout NT scripture to share financially the same way. The enemy cannot undo the accomplishments of our resurrected Lord. So, he tries to get us to reject them by getting us to accept the doctrine of another covenant. But ours is the new, eternal covenant that Lord Jesus gave His life to establish for God's children. God's NT Church's DNA is Volunteerism, produced by God's love.

141

www.ingramcontent.com/pod-product-compliance
Lightning Source LLC
LaVergne TN
LVHW041224080426
835508LV00011B/1072